Table of Contents

Introduction 7

Getting Acquainted with God. 11

Unwavering Faith 33

Prayer and Unforgiveness 55

Why Healing Belongs to Us 79

Different Kinds of Prayers. 93

Our Words are Powerful 107

Believers Have Authority Over Satan 121

The Rapture and Tribulation 135

Conclusion 149

Eight-Week Bible Study 151

Introduction

It hurts my heart to see the anti-Christian attitude of most news media, TV programming, Hollywood celebrities and producers, and talk show hosts who make fun of God and constantly put Christians down; they distort history and the life and mission of Jesus for the money it brings them. I heard a TV talk show host actually yell, "It's just a religion! Go to commercial!" right over a Christian who was speaking. Another TV host actually said that Christians were worse than terrorists, but when a guest on the show said something about the Muslim terrorists that caused 9/11, two of these same hosts walked off the set. This kind of behavior is becoming more and more prevalent in today's society because people are putting biased political correctness and their own personal worldly preferences before the principles of the God who made them.

I started writing this book when my children were teenagers, but I felt compelled to continue writing for other teens, young adults, and all who haven't gotten acquainted with God yet. I have been a believer since I was very young, and in my journey growing closer and closer to God, I have had many life-changing personal experiences, which I would like to share so you will understand how vital it is to draw close to God. Don't wait until there is trouble in your life and you desperately need help to look for God.

God works in our lives only when we submit ourselves to Him. God has given each of us free will, and He will only intervene when we ask Him to. God is waiting for you to draw near to Him and ask for His help. God's Spirit is everywhere, but until you know Him through your spirit, you will not be able to recognize or understand many things. God said, "My people are dying for lack of knowledge."

Whether you are questioning God, you are a new believer, or have been a Christian all your life, this book will answer your questions and strengthen your relationship with God. Now is the time to get acquainted with Him.

Getting Acquainted with God

God desires a close relationship with each of us. I know that might be hard for some people to believe, but that is truly why He created us. We are His creation, and the desire of God's heart is to have a close relationship with each of us no matter where we are in our lives. He is waiting for each of us to draw near to Him, but He will not force us to come to Him. We must draw near to God of our own free will and get acquainted with Him through His Spirit. God's Spirit is everywhere, but until you know Him through His Spirit, you will not be able to recognize or understand many things.

Many people blame God instead of Satan for everything bad that happens in the world. It is really surprising how many people don't understand that this world is Satan's territory, and as long as we are in it, Satan will try to attack us. The only way you can defend yourself against Satan is to draw near to God and His Son. God created the world to operate under the laws that He (God) set in motion when He created it, but the laws governing the earth today very largely came into being with the fall of man through Adam and Eve's disobedience, the curse upon the earth by Satan, and the mistreatment of the earth by humans themselves.

Some people question the Bible because it doesn't conform to their scientific principles, but God will never be confined by scientific ways of doing things, because His ways are far superior, above and beyond anything that we could ever imagine. God's infinite power and ability will never be confined in a scientific box. "For My thoughts are not your thoughts, neither are your ways My ways," says the Lord. "For as the heavens are higher than the earth, so are My ways higher than your ways, and My thoughts than your thoughts." God is not just a religion. I can show you how to prove for yourself that God is alive and full of power. Nobody would doubt there is a God if they would just take the time to get acquainted with Him.

There are people living without God because they think they can do everything in their own strength and/or with their money. But they are kidding themselves, because the devil is in the world trying to destroy each of us. God gave each of us free will to make our own decisions, and He is not running around playing Superman in everybody's lives. Yes, He has the power to do that, but He doesn't force people to do what He wants them to do. If He did, then everyone would be a Christian. God loves every one of us, and He has made provisions for all of us, but we must be willing to possess what is ours. God works in our lives only when we submit ourselves to Him.

It doesn't matter what you have done in your life. God will receive you just as you are, and He restores favor to those who choose Him. God will work on your behalf as you ask Him to, but He will not force people to come to Him. It is our choice to make. By failing to believe who we are in Christ and what we possess in Christ, we can allow Satan to gain the upper hand in our situation.

When we draw near to God and humble ourselves in His presence, He will come close to us. God's love covers everybody in the world, but He will not force people to choose Him over Satan. If we think that we don't need God because we can do it on our own and we turn our back on Him, we are opening the door to the devil and his destruction.

Some people may have tried to understand God and the things of God with their mind and intellect, but when they don't find God their way, they claim that there is no God. What they don't realize is that you can't get acquainted with God by what you see or by your emotions, but by your spirit coming into contact with God's Spirit and His Word. The real knowledge and wisdom of God takes place in your spirit or heart, not in your mind or intellect. God definitely is not just a religion, and if you will come along with me, I will introduce you to Him.

I do not just hope there is a God; I know Him and His Son, Jesus. I don't have to see my God to know he is near me any more than I have to see the air to know it is there. I can't see the wind, but I can feel it and see the effects of it. My God is not just a religion, and I don't just blindly believe in a doctrine that was passed down to me. I have talked to my God and heard His reply. I feel His great love and continual presence. I have seen the results of my urgent prayers and the work of His angels, who guard my loved ones and me. I know my God, His Son, and His Spirit personally. I know without a doubt that God loves me, guides me, talks to me, strengthens me, warns me, teaches me through my spirit, keeps His mighty angels around me, and fills me with His discernment and peace.

One of the first things we learn is that God is a spirit. It is true. God is a spirit, and He exists everywhere in the world simultaneously and can also communicate with us one on one. God is the creator of all things, but God created only man in His image, male and female, and breathed His Spirit into them and blessed them. That means that we have a body that lives in the world; we have a soul that is our mind, will, and emotions; and we have a spirit—from God. God is a personal God who loves all His children, and each of us can talk to Him whenever we choose—no matter where we are. That's how big God is.

It is important to get to know who God is in the same way you would get to know anyone else—by getting acquainted with Him. In order to get acquainted with someone, you must listen to him and hear what he says. To get acquainted with God, you must read His Word, pray and talk to Him, and also listen to Him. Listening for God is hard sometimes when we feel desperate or anxious, so we talk too much and don't take the time to listen, but reading and studying God's Word is a form of listening to Him. You will never hear God talk to you until you are quiet long enough for His Spirit to speak to your spirit, but that is not the only way God communicates with us.

We need to get acquainted with God in an intimate Father-child relationship. We humans must realize that we are spirits (in God's likeness). We have a soul and we live in a body. People would not doubt that there is a God if they would just take the time to get acquainted with Him through their spirit.

I have been telling you that you need to draw near to God so He will draw near you. Here is an example of how he communicated with me in a loving way, even though I wasn't in a loving mood. One day, after a particularly hectic morning getting my children off to school, I glanced in the mirror, as I was about to walk out the door. As I put my hand up to my hair, I accidentally touched my metal glasses and they fell apart. My glasses had constantly been falling apart ever since I bought them, so I called the eye doctor's office. I told the receptionist that I didn't have an appointment but I was coming over right now, so they could put my glasses back together again so I could go to work. I was very angry and even angry with God. All the way to the eye doctor's office, I was yelling at God. I told Him that I didn't believe He even knew that my children and I were down here. I told Him I knew he didn't hear my prayers and He probably didn't even care about what happened to us anyway, and so on. When I got to the eye doctor's office, I gave my glasses to the receptionist and picked up a magazine and sat down to read it. As I opened the magazine, a card fell out of it into my lap. I picked it up and read it. Everything I had yelled at God about was answered in the Bible verses on the card. I quickly prayed and asked God to forgive me for yelling at him. I still have the card. (This experience taught me that my God is a loving Father and loves me unconditionally.)

Here is another example of how God has communicated with me:

One day when I was talking to God, I told Him that I didn't know if the writing I felt compelled to do was just for my children and me or for Him. I challenged God to give me words right then if it was His will for me to write for Him, and immediately, He filled my head with His words. That's how quickly God answered my prayer. I actually saw the words in my head just as they are written below.

> Whenever I want to talk to My Father,
> I knock, and Jesus opens the door.
>
> I walk from the darkness into the light,
> And I feel their love surrounding me.
>
> As we talk, they lift my burdens from me.
> They comfort me and tell me to rest.
>
> I'm hungry, and My Father feeds me His Word,
> Which strengthens me and fills me with peace.

I can't even put into words how this experience drew me closer to God and really strengthened my faith and confidence in my walk with God.

When we draw near to God and humble ourselves in His presence, He comes close to us and hears and answers our prayers. We are supposed to be strong in the Lord (be empowered through our union with Him) and draw our strength from Him. God loves every one of us, and He has made provisions for all of us, but we must be willing to possess what is ours. God works in our lives only when we submit ourselves to Him. Then God will work on our behalf as we ask Him to. When you receive Jesus as your Savior, God becomes your Father and cares for you with an everlasting love.

> God said, "My people are destroyed for lack of knowledge, because thou hast rejected knowledge, I will also reject thee. Seeing thou hast forgotten the law of thy God, I will also forget thy children." (I would say this is God's way of telling us to come close to Him and understand the knowledge He wants to give us, because we could be destroyed by Satan without the knowledge from God.)
>
> Hosea 4:6, KJV

Not only is God telling us to come close to Him, but He is also telling us that He will empower us with His strength when we do. "Be strong in the Lord [be empowered through your union with Him]; draw your strength from Him [that strength which His boundless might provides]." Ephesians 6:10–13

God fashioned and made this tiny little planet called earth. He did not create it to be empty, but He formed the earth to be inhabited by the human race, as the Bible tells us. God created only man in His image, male and female, breathed His Spirit into them, and blessed them. God did not breathe His Spirit into any animal, fish, bird, or tree. God created the earth and everything on it and around it to support human life; the earth has unique animals to feed and clothe us, unique plants for healing and eating, unique birds, reptiles, and insects, each with a unique purpose. All of this is God's creation. No big bang did that.

It is beyond my comprehension how anyone could possibly believe that all the wonderful things in this world just happened to appear without any design, a world with each person uniquely different from all others, proven by our fingerprints and DNA. How could that be random?

God made the world and the fullness thereof; and it was good, and there was nothing that was bad. Then God made Adam and gave him dominion over all the work of His hands (the earth and everything on it). But when Adam and Eve sinned, all mankind fell heir to the terrible results. God created the world to operate under the laws that He (God) set in motion when He created it, but the laws governing the earth today very largely came into being with the fall of man through Adam and Eve's disobedience, the curse upon the earth by Satan, and the mistreatment of the earth by humans themselves.

I have heard many people blame God for accidents, sickness, pain, death, storms, floods, earthquakes, and other catastrophes. They say that God is a cruel God, but these things are from the devil, not God. If God caused the sickness and storms, then Jesus would not have gone against His Father's will to heal and rebuke them. Since Jesus had subjected His own will entirely to that of His Father at the River Jordan, there was nothing in Jesus that would go against His Father's will. It was God's will for

Jesus to heal the sick, cast out demons, raise people from the dead, and rebuke storms, because they come from Satan, not God.

John 3:17 says, "For God did not send the Son into the world in order to judge the world, but that the world might find salvation and be made safe and sound through Him." If God were the author of sickness and disease and God healed people through Jesus, then God worked against Himself; and if God caused the storm, God would be working against himself by causing it to cease. This cannot be, for Jesus said, "If a kingdom be divided against itself, that kingdom cannot stand and if a house be divided against itself, that house cannot stand" (Mark 3:24–25, KJV).

Our opposition in this life comes from the spiritual realm, and we are to take our stand on the Word of God and enforce our victory against Satan. Satan is the one roaming this world like a lion looking for those he can destroy. Satan is the father of lies and destruction and death. This world is Satan's territory, and as long as we are in it, Satan will try to attack us. The only way you can defend yourself against Satan is to draw close to God and His Son Jesus. The Bible tells us that God sends His angels to protect those who believe in Him.

Every day, I ask God to keep His angels around my loved ones and me, and I know in my heart that they constantly watch over us because I have had many experiences that couldn't have happened the way they did without angels intervening for us. For example, a few years ago, I was about to walk down the stairs in my home with my arms full of picture frames and a toolbox in my other arm. I wasn't holding onto the railing, and I lost my balance as I stepped off the top step and was thrown forward down the stairs. I know that God's angels had me in their arms, because I didn't even hit one step on the way down, but ended up hanging upside down holding onto the railing thirteen steps below, just above the landing. The picture frames that I was going to hang up and the tools that I had been carrying were all over the place. There was broken glass and broken frames and tools everywhere on the steps, but I was fine. There is no doubt in my mind that I could have died in that fall down those stairs or at least been seriously injured, but I was not even jostled around. I believe I was caught by the angels that God keeps around me every day, because there is no other way I can explain falling all that way down a full flight of wooden stairs and not even hitting one step. Yes, I believe in God's mighty angels, and I thank Him for them every day.

For example: My boss had to fly out of town for a meeting and we heard on the news that the plane she was in was having trouble with the landing gear. The plane was having to circle around the airport in order to get rid of the excess gasoline so it could try to land as safely as possible. The plane had to circle the airport for almost an hour, so there was plenty of time to pray and also call others to pray for the safe landing of the plane. I was not worried about it because after I prayed, I had a peaceful feeling and I knew in my spirit that everything would be okay. However, one young woman who worked with me was getting frantic about it, so I told her that there were many people praying for this plane and I was sure there were many angels around it so it would land safely. (She rolled her eyes and looked at me like I was crazy.) The plane landed just as it would have if its wheels were down, and everyone was safe with no injuries. The angels did a great job.

Another example: My sister was driving down a country road at dusk. She went over the top of a hill and there was a tractor with bright lights on it pulled across the road with a piece of farm equipment, with lots of sharp prongs on it, in the middle of the road. She couldn't stop her truck in time and pointed prongs from the farm equipment came through the front of her truck. One prong would have gone into her face, but she saw a very large man put his hand up to stop the prong, and his body must have shielded the other prongs that would have hit her other places. She said the prongs on the passenger side of her truck went all the way through the back of the seat. When I asked her to describe him she said, he was very large, wore a white robe that the tractor lights seemed to go through, he was bald, and he looked like Mr. Clean to her. She said that he was gone as quickly as he appeared. (What a great way to meet your guardian angel.)

God is yearning for you to come close to Him, receive His Son, and believe His Word. Then the only way God will let go of you is if you let go of Him of your own free will and turn your back on Him. If you have let go of God, I pray that you will sincerely ask God to forgive you and take His hand again and hold on for dear life. By failing to believe the Word of God and failing to exercise our authority in Christ against the devil, we allow Satan to gain the upper hand in our lives.

We must recognize that we are disloyal to God when we do not honor and revere Him as the God of the universe. God loves every one of us, and He has made provisions for all of us, but we must be willing to possess what is ours.

I believe we are to ask our Father, in the name of Jesus, for anything that does not go against His Word. When I have a problem that just seems to be getting worse no matter what I do, I pray: "Dear Father, I love You and praise You and thank You for all You do for me and my family. I lift myself up to You and ask You to take over this (explain the situation or problem) because I can't fix it on my own. I give it to You, and I let go and let God. I thank You that my prayer is being answered, and I praise You for it! I pray in Jesus' Name. Amen." (When I pray, I believe, without doubting, that what I asked for is taken care of and I go about my day without worrying, because God is my Father and He is doing everything I asked Him to do. I let go and let God.)

When we pray God still heals terminally ill people that the doctors have given up on. Doctors and many millions of others have seen the miracles and have documented many cases where there is no scientific explanation for their healing. But with God, all things are possible. I believe that we all have seen His miracles in our lives but might not have recognized them as such. Miracles are not just in healing, and healing doesn't have to be life threatening for you to pray and receive your miracle. There have been many times in my life that I have prayed over little things and big problems and immediately seen results.

Many times, I have prayed for God's protection before I started driving on a trip, and later, a car would be about to hit us but miss hitting us by just a hair when it seemed impossible that it could miss us at all. Other times when I have prayed for protection, I knew without a doubt that there were angels surrounding us not because I could see them, but I just knew in my spirit and had a peace in me. Sometimes the Holy Spirit intercedes to warn me or bring something up in my mind that helps me. And yes, there are times when I haven't paid attention to my spirit but later realized that if I had, things would have happened differently.

The more time you spend reading and studying the Bible, praying, and talking to God, the more you will understand and your faith will grow. I have personalized Bible prayers and prayed them frequently to strengthen my faith, discernment, understanding and knowledge of God to help me draw closer to Him. I recommend this for everyone to do, because it works. Here are a few Bible prayers I recommend you personalize and pray for yourself by changing the words from *you, your*, and personalize them to *I, me*, and *my*, to help you draw closer to God and grow in your faith. (Ephesians 1:17–23, Ephesians 3:14–21, and Mark 11:22–25.)

For example: Take the prayer in Ephesians 3:14–21 and change the words from *you, your*, and personalize them to *I, me*, and *my* … then pray the prayer at least once a day, but more frequently if you can. As you pray, really concentrate on the words and what they mean and take them for your own.

I bow my knees before the Father of our Lord Jesus Christ, for whom every family in heaven and on earth is named. May He grant *me* out of the rich treasury of His glory to be strengthened and reinforced with mighty power in the inner man by the Holy Spirit Himself indwelling *my* innermost being and personality. May Christ through *my* faith actually dwell, settle down, abide, and make His permanent home in *my* heart. May *I* be rooted deep in love and founded securely on love. That *I* may have the power and be strong to apprehend and grasp with all the saints what is the breadth and length and height and depth of it. That *I* may really come to know personally, through experience for *myself*, the love of Christ, which far surpasses mere knowledge. That *I* may be filled through all *my* being unto all the fullness of God, may *I* have the richest measure of the divine Presence, and become a body wholly filled and flooded with God Himself. Now to Him Who, by the power that is at work within *me*, is able to carry out His purpose and do superabundantly, far over and above all that *I* dare ask or think (infinitely beyond *my* highest prayers, desires, thoughts, hopes, or dreams). To Him be the glory in the church and in Christ Jesus throughout all generations forever and ever. Amen

We now live in the day of grace, and God's grace is simple. We all have a choice to get acquainted with God, His Son, His Spirit, and His Word … or refuse to accept Jesus and stay in the darkness of the world. If we choose the world instead of God and His Son, we are turning our back on God of our own free will and we align ourselves with Satan, who is already the defeated foe of God.

If you align yourself against the God who created you, then you are aligning yourself on the side of Satan of your own free will. You have to be careful who or what you put as the top priority in your life. If you idolize money, athletes, celebrities, drinking, drugs, sex, or put any of your personal preferences before the God of this world, you are being a friend to the world, not God.

Whether you believe it or not, everything in the Bible will come to pass and every one of us will have to bow down before the Lord. At that time, it will be too late to change your mind. Whether you believe it or not God's Word is the law of this universe. Without Jesus, you have no access to God and no access to heaven, so you stay in the darkness of the world under the control of Satan.

God's grace is simple. Believe in the God of the Bible and His Word; receive His Son, Jesus, into your heart; ask for forgiveness for your sins; and forgive all who have trespassed against you. If you have not received Jesus as your Savior and would like to, pray the following prayer:

> Dear heavenly Father, I believe in my heart and I confess with my mouth that God raised His Son, Jesus, from the grave for my salvation and healing, and I receive Jesus as my Lord and Savior. I ask forgiveness for my sins, and I let go of the anger and unforgiveness that I've been holding and I forgive all those who have trespassed against me. I pray in Jesus' name. Amen.

When my granddaughter was young, she asked me why I love God so much, and this is what I told her: God is my Father, and Jesus is my Brother, and I am filled with their Spirit and love, just as you are, because we have received Jesus as our Savior. I believe what God's Word says, and my faith will not waver because I know that God is with me and will never leave me. I feel His love and I see what His love does. I have peace in my life that passes all understanding and His Spirit lives in me, as He does in you. The Holy Spirit in us is greater than the devil that roams the world, so we don't have to be afraid of the devil because God's angels fight for us. Remember when you're sick that Jesus already won our healing at the cross—not just our salvation—and we need to claim our healing in the Name of Jesus. We belong to God and His power works through us. God was the Holy Spirit in Jesus, and now He is the Holy Spirit in those of us who believe in Him. As you grow older, remember these teachings and learn to strengthen your own faith, never doubt that God loves you, will answer your prayers, and keep His mighty angels around you when you ask Him to. (This is my advice to everyone.)

Unwavering Faith

I believe that too many people are just hoping they will receive healing or answer to their prayers, but it is not hope that gets the job done. Hope is always future tense... pointing to the future. Hope believes in a promise, but faith believes in the one who promises. Faith gives substance to our hope. *Faith is laying hold of the unrealities of hope and bringing them into the realm of reality... by faith.*

My definition of Christianity is a life system of faith in touch with the living God of the universe, His Son, Jesus; His Spirit; and His Word. The Blood of Jesus, the Name of Jesus, and the Word of God are all-powerful, but it takes faith to set this power to working.

> Faith is the assurance (the confirmation, the title deed) of the things we hope for, being the proof of things we do not see and the conviction of their reality [faith perceiving as real fact what is not revealed to the senses]. By faith, we understand that the worlds were framed (fashioned, put in order, and equipped for their intended purpose), by the Word of God so that what we see was not made out of things which are visible.
>
> Hebrews 11:1, 3

Faith is a simple trust and confidence in God and His Word. Believe and stand firm in faith, thanking and praising the Lord for your healing or the answer to any of your prayers even before you can see it in reality. Remember, without faith, it is impossible to please God; so pray in the Name of Jesus, plead the Blood of Jesus over your loved ones and you, and stand firm in faith without wavering in your confession of faith in God's Word and His power.

God loves all of us and He has made provisions for all of us, but we must be willing to possess what is ours. If a person does not want to hear and know the Word of God, they cannot have faith. But by studying the Word of God for yourself, you can gain knowledge of what is yours in Him. We must think and believe and confess things in line with the Word of God, because we cannot believe beyond the actual knowledge we have.

Remember, God said, "My people are dying for lack of knowledge."

> For without faith it is impossible to please and be satisfactory to Him. For whoever would come near to God must believe that God exists and that He is the rewarder of those who earnestly and diligently seek Him.
>
> Hebrews 11:6

In the Old Testament, God gave the people rules to live by, and He told them what would happen to them if they didn't live by His rules. Even though the people actually saw God do miracles and send manna from heaven daily and part the Red Sea, they still didn't live by His principles, but by their own sinful human preferences. They knew that God said He would bring plagues, pestilence, and even death on them if they didn't obey. What a surprise it must have been to them that they suffered the consequences of their actions. The human race was separated from God by its sin.

The God of the Old Testament is the same powerful God as the God of the New Testament, but God has done away with His Old Covenant with man and replaced it with the New Covenant of God's grace to all mankind. If you believe in the God of the universe, then you must also believe in His Son, Jesus, because our only access to God is through His Son. Without Jesus we are estranged from God.

In the Scripture verses below it is talking about the first order, which is the Old Covenant, and the second order, which is the New Covenant with God.

> Hence, when He [Christ] entered into the world, He said, Sacrifices and offerings You have not desired, but instead You have made ready a body for Me [to offer]; In burnt offerings You have taken no delight. Then I said, Behold, here I am, coming to do Your

will, O God ... [to fulfill] what is written of
Me in the volume of the Book (Ps 40:6–8).

He then went on to say, Behold, I am
coming to do your will. Thus He does away
with and annuls the first (former) order [as
a means of expiating sin] so that He might
inaugurate and establish the second order. And
in accordance with this will [of God] we have
been made holy (consecrated and sanctified)
through the offering, made once, for all of the
body of Jesus Christ (the Anointed One).

Hebrews 10:5, 9–10

Jesus died for us, Jesus took our sins, Jesus took
our infirmities and bore our sicknesses, Jesus delivered us from the authority of darkness (Satan and
his demons), and Jesus redeemed us and made us
new creatures that we might become the righteousness of God through Jesus. Christ Jesus is the head
of the church and believers are members of the body
of Christ.

Satan's dominion over us is broken only when we
receive redemption in Jesus Christ. That means Satan
loses his dominion over our lives the minute we are
born again, and Jesus Christ becomes our Lord. Jesus

is the key to our direct access to God, so until we accept Jesus as our Savior and ask forgiveness of our sins, we are still separated from God, and Satan has dominion over us.

We must understand that God's Spirit was in Jesus, reconciling the world unto Him. Jesus does not have to die again to save anybody, because He already died for all of us, once and for all, to legally provide our redemption, but we just have to receive the salvation that is a gift to us. That which the Lord has legally purchased and provided for us becomes ours when we believe the Word of God in our heart and confess that it is true and that it is ours. If a person sins after he has been born again, he does not need to be born again time after time. A person can only be born again once, but he can be forgiven of his sins many, many times.

Since Christ had subjected His own will entirely to that of the Father at the River Jordan, there was nothing in Him that would go against His Father's will. That is when Jesus started healing the sick and teaching the Word of God to everyone who would listen, but Jesus was able to do nothing of Himself, only as God worked through Him. When Jesus became man, it was so He could teach and intercede for the human race. While Jesus walked on earth, He healed the sick, rebuked the storms, cast out demons, and did other miracles. Jesus taught His followers that they could intercede for others as long as they had faith to believe what He taught them, and when He rose from the earth His Spirit was with them, as it is with believers today.

Jesus said:

> If a person [really] loves Me, he will keep My Word [obey my teaching]; and My Father will love him, and We will come to him and make Our home (abode, special dwelling place) with him.
>
> John 14:23

God took Satan's authority away from him when He raised Jesus from the grave and gave us victory over death and authority over the devil through Christ Jesus. By the power of God, Jesus was raised from the grave and the veil between heaven and earth was torn down, which means that we now have direct access to God through Jesus and there is no priest or temple or anyone standing between Jesus and us.

Jesus took back our authority on earth, and Jesus took our sins and sicknesses, infirmities, grief, and pain on Himself so we would not have to suffer them. But we have a part to play. We are separated from God by our sins until we accept Jesus, as our Savior, and ask forgiveness for our sins.

We can have direct access to God only through His Son, Jesus. When we receive Jesus into our hearts as our Lord and Savior, His Spirit abides in us to guide and teach us. We all can know God and have a relationship with Him through Jesus, His Word, and His Spirit, but we must remember that Jesus is the key.

In the Bible verses below Jesus tells us that the thief (Satan) comes only in order to steal, kill, and destroy, but Jesus gave His life willingly for the human race, so we may have and enjoy a full and abundant life.

Jesus said:

> I am the door; anyone who enters in through me will be saved (will live). He will come in and he will go out (freely), and will find pasture. The thief comes only in order to steal, kill, and destroy. I came that they may

have and enjoy life, and have it in abundance (to the full, till it overflows.) I am the Good Shepherd. The Good Shepherd risks and lays down His [own] life for the sheep.

John 10:9–11

The promise to believers is:

If we [freely] admit that we have sinned and confess our sins, he is faithful and just (true to His own nature and promises) and will forgive our sins and [continuously] cleanse us from all unrighteousness [everything not in conformity to His will in purpose, thought, and action].

1 John 1:9

Jesus said

I assure you, most solemnly, I tell you that unless a person is born again (anew, from above), he cannot ever see (know, be acquainted with, and experience) the kingdom of God.

John 3:3

Jesus is the key to us receiving God's grace, forgiveness, protection, guidance, and a best friend forever. Jesus gave His life willingly as the last sacrifice so the human race could get out from under Satan's authority in this world. Jesus was God's perfect gift to mankind, because without Jesus interceding for us, we could not escape from the rule of Satan in the world.

Jesus said:

> Keep on asking and it will be given you; keep on seeking and you will find; keep on knocking [reverently] and [the door] will be opened to you. For everyone who keeps on asking receives; and he who keeps on seeking finds; and to him who keeps on knocking, [the door] will be opened.
>
> Matthew 7:7–8

We must have faith in what God has said in His Word and exercise our testimony against the devil in faith that this will cause the devil to flee from us because God's Word says so. Having true faith means we believe that the devil and the disease (or problem) have gone, that healing (or the answer to the problem) takes its place, and that we are well because the Blood of Jesus overcomes the devil and destroys his work.

God has given us the Blood of Jesus and says it overcomes Satan as we testify to its power, which means that it will rob the devil of his power to harm us, but only if we stand firm in faith, believing that we are healed (or the problem is taken care of). We must plant our feet and stand firm in faith, resisting the devil and standing on the Word of God, and never waver from our firm stance of faith until victory comes.

We are supposed to have faith constantly and resist the devil, even when our natural eyes tell us that we are still sick or the problem is still there, because in the Spirit, healing (or answer to our problem) is on its way to us. We must have faith in our hearts to believe, and confess with our mouths what God's Word says.

This world is Satan's territory, and as long as we are in it, he will try to attack us. For that reason, believers should daily ask God to cover them with the Blood of Jesus, surround them with His angels, and stand firm believing that Satan cannot harm them. We must truly believe in faith that the Blood of Jesus, His Name, and God's Word takes from Satan all power to put anything on us or to keep anything on us, because God (who cannot lie) says these things overcome the devil every time.

The Bible verse below tells us everything that we need to know to pray and get results from God, but it also tells us that we have to stand in faith, not doubting or wavering. When you pray this prayer, you should substitute whatever the problem or sickness is for the word *mountain*, because we are supposed to speak to the sickness or problem and tell it to be lifted up and cast into the sea! You can also plead the Blood of Jesus against the sickness or problem and claim, in the Name of Jesus, that the problem must flee now!

> Jesus said, "Have faith in God [constantly]. Truly I tell you, whoever says to this mountain, be lifted up and cast into the sea! And does not doubt at all in his heart, but believes that what he says will take place, it will be done for him. For this reason I am telling you, whatever you ask in prayer, believe (trust and be confident) that it is granted to you and you will get it.

And whenever you stand praying, if you have anything against anyone, forgive him and let it drop (leave it, let it go), in order that your Father Who is in heaven may also forgive you your [own] failings and shortcomings and let them drop. But if you do not forgive, neither will your Father in heaven forgive your failings and shortcomings.

Mark 11:22–26

God's will is for us to be healthy and prosperous and have an abundant life. That's why He sent Jesus to show us how much He loves us. If you need more faith, ask Him to strengthen your faith. Pray that God would open the eyes of your heart and flood you with His wisdom, discernment, and the knowledge of Him and do not doubt that He wants you healed, prosperous, and living in peace.

You can be a good person, but if you haven't received Jesus, as your Savior and been born again, Satan has authority over you. God could have just zapped Satan and his demon followers out of the world. But if He did that, He would have been violating His own laws of the universe. In order for God to take away Satan's authority over the world, He had

to send a man into the world to take back the authority that Satan had stolen from Adam and Eve (and
the entire human race). We were sold into sin and
spiritual death (through Adam and Eve) and Satan
had dominion over us, because the earth became
Satan's territory.

Our confessions of faith should be:

I belong to Christ Jesus, and Satan no longer has
dominion to rule over me unless I let him, so I confess
from my heart, out of my mouth: Sin, sickness, weakness, disease, and poverty have no dominion over me
anymore. Greater is the Holy Spirit in me than the
devil that is in the world. I overcome Satan by the
Blood of the Lamb and the word of my testimony.

Jesus said:

> If you [really] love me you will keep (obey)
> my commandments and I will ask the Father
> and He will give you another Comforter,
> (Counselor, Helper, Intercessor, Advocate,
> Strengthener, and Standby), that He may
> remain with you forever. The Spirit of Truth,
> Whom the world cannot receive (welcome,
> take to its heart), because it does not see
> Him or know and recognize Him. But you

know and recognize Him, for He lives with you [constantly] and will be in you. I will not leave you as orphans [comfortless, desolate, bereaved, forlorn, helpless]; I will come [back] to you. Just a little while now, and the world will not see me any more, but you will see me; because I live, you will live also. At that time you will know [for yourselves] that I am in My Father, and you are in me, and I [am] in you. The person who has my commands and keeps them is the one who [really] loves me, and whoever [really] loves me will be loved by My Father, and I [too] will love him and will show (reveal, manifest) Myself to him. [I will let Myself be clearly seen by him and make Myself real to him.]

John 14:15–21

The Spirit Whom He has caused to dwell in us yearns over us and He yearns, with a jealous love, for His Spirit to be welcomed by us. But He gives us more and more grace (power of the Holy Spirit, to meet this evil tendency and all others fully). This is why He says: God sets Himself against the proud and haughty, but gives grace [continually] to the lowly (those that are humble enough to receive it). So be subject to God. Resist the devil [stand firm against him] and he will flee from you. Come close to God and He will come close to you. [Recognize that you are] sinners, get your soiled hands clean; [realize that you have been disloyal] wavering individuals with divided interests, and purify your hearts [of your spiritual adultery].

James 4:5–8

Our confession should be:

No man shall take me out of God's hands for I have eternal life. I let the peace of God rule in my heart and I refuse to worry about anything. God is on my side, God is in me now, who can be against me? I am of God and have overcome Satan, for greater is the Holy Spirit is in me than the devil that is in the world.

Lean on, trust in, and be confident in the Lord with all your heart and mind and do not rely on your own insight or understanding. In all your ways know, recognize, and acknowledge Him, and He will direct and make straight and plain your paths. Be not wise in your own eyes; reverently fear and worship the Lord and turn [entirely] away from evil.

Proverbs 3:5–8

The spirit and the soul are not the same. With our body, we see the physical realm; with our soul, we feel the intellectual and emotional; with our spirit, we contact the spiritual realm and we sense the Holy Spirit.

The Holy Spirit in us will give us discernment about things we could not possibly know about otherwise. For example, I woke up from a sound sleep one night and knew in my spirit that my youngest son was in trouble. I tried to call him on his cell phone, but he didn't answer. I started praying for his safety, and I continued to pray for him until I got a peaceful feeling within me. Only then did I try to sleep again. A little later, he called me to tell me he had an accident but he was okay. (I knew in my spirit that he was okay before he called, and this is not the only time this has happened to me with my children.)

Sometimes I get a heavy feeling in my heart and somebody's face will keep coming to my mind, and I know that I have to pray for that person even though

I don't know exactly what I'm praying about. But I pray until I get a peaceful, calm feeling.

I also know that parents have a special duty to pray over their children, because even though our children tune us out sometimes, they can't tune out our prayers, and our prayers for our children are a high priority with God.

For example, one of my sons was running around at school with a boy who didn't like authority and I didn't approve of, but nothing I said to my son seemed to make a difference. So I prayed that God would get them away from each other at school, and He soon did.

My children are grown up now, but I still pray for them each day because I am still their parent and my prayers for them are still a priority to God. For example, one of my sons was laid off and had been looking for a good job for a long time. I prayed and asked God to give him "the best job he's ever had" as soon as possible. Then I praised and thanked God for doing what I asked, and I knew He was answering my prayer. My son called me a couple days later and said, "Mom, this afternoon I have the second interview for 'the best job I've ever had,' and I think I'm going to get it." He got the job. God is true to His Word.

Every spiritual law and faith principle that God set forth in His Word was for our benefit. We can have what we say when we learn to release faith from the heart in our words. The Word of God conceived in our heart and spoken out of our mouth is really powerful. We should train ourselves to speak God's Word and use His Word to defeat Satan as Jesus did.

Jesus said:

> If any man is thirsty, let him come to Me and drink! He who believes in Me, [who cleaves to and trusts in and relies on Me] as the Scripture has said, from his innermost being shall flow [continuously] springs and rivers of living water. But He was speaking here of the Spirit, Whom those who believed (trusted, had faith) in Him were afterward to receive. For the [Holy] Spirit had not yet been given, because Jesus was not yet glorified (raised to honor).
>
> John 7:37–39

God created the universe by His words. Man is created in the image of God, so we are supposed to release our faith in words. Man is a physical, mental, and spiritual being. The Word of God conceived in our human spirit and spoken out of our mouth becomes power that works for us. God's Word is full of power, but His Word is powerless when left unspoken. Jesus told us to attend to His words, for they are life and health to all our flesh.

The Word of God has been given to us so our thinking can be in line with the Bible, because we cannot believe beyond our actual knowledge of God's Word. We need to have Bible faith, which means that we need to know what God's Word says and we must get it inside of our hearts, so we know without a doubt that God wants us to prosper and be in good health. We must speak the Word of God about things "that be not as though they are" and confess victory in the face of apparent defeat, confess abundance in the face of apparent lack, and confess healing and health in the face of sickness.

The Bible is God's living Word to each of us, so our thinking, believing, and confessing must be in line with God's Word. Jesus told us to attend to His words, for they are life and health to all our flesh. Jesus gave us the authority and the power to use the Word of God for our benefit, but in order for it to be effective, we must speak it (in faith) out of our mouth. God's Word is true and full of power, but His Word is powerless when left unspoken, so we must start believing and speaking the Word and standing in faith even when we cannot see results in the natural. When we pray and speak the Word of God from our hearts (in faith), it will produce peace, prosperity, health, and healing.

It is important for us to know what God, through His Word and through the Holy Spirit, has done for us and for us to know what our Lord, Jesus Christ, is doing for us now as He sits at the right hand of our Father, God, in heaven. We are supposed to fearlessly, confidently, and boldly draw near to the throne of God's grace and receive mercy for our failures and find grace to help for every need. When Christ died and was raised from the dead, He paid for every sin—past, present, and future—and to think otherwise is to proclaim His work on the cross as insufficient. It is a true gift with no strings attached and is permanently ours. We can know for sure that we have eternal life through God's promises in Scripture and the witness of the Holy Spirit within us.

Prayer and Unforgiveness

Everything we pray about—healing, depression, finances, and so on—all has to come to pass in the natural world, and Satan is at work here. It is vital that people realize that it is Satan who is trying to keep our prayers from being answered, not God. Satan will try to block our blessings any way he can to keep them from coming to us. When there is the least delay, some people think maybe God doesn't want them to have what they have prayed for. They mistakenly blame God when they should recognize that the source of all opposition is Satan.

It is important for us to realize it is the prayer of faith that releases God's wisdom, discernment, knowledge, and power into our situation and does the impossible for us. Our prayers are important because God is waiting for us to ask before He will intervene in our lives. God is yearning for you to draw near to Him and Jesus, so He can help you, but He will not force you to come to Him.

We can get confidence, boldness, and faith when we read and study God's Word. Our prayers are always supposed to be based on God's will in His Word and never to contain the word *if*, because *if* is not faith. The Bible tells us to cast our cares on the Lord and teaches us to humbly pray a heartfelt, fervent, earnest request for ourselves and for God's people. But we also have a responsibility to pray for unbelievers and all those in authority.

God promises to hear our prayers and grant us anything we ask in Jesus' Name as long as it is in line with the Bible. This simply means that we shouldn't ask for something immoral or harmful that God would not want us to have.

In Mark 11:22–25, Jesus teaches us how to pray to get our prayers answered:

Have faith in God [constantly]. Truly I tell you, whoever says to this mountain, Be lifted up and cast into the sea! And does not doubt at all in his heart, but believes that what he says will take place, it will be done for him. For this reason I am telling you, whatever you ask in prayer, believe (trust and be confident) that it is granted to you and you will get it. And whenever you stand praying, if you have anything against anyone, forgive him and let it drop (leave it, let it go), in order that your Father Who is in heaven may also forgive you your [own] failings and shortcomings and let them drop. But if you do not forgive, neither will your Father in heaven forgive your failings and shortcomings. (When Jesus is talking about speaking to the mountain ... He means problem or sickness. So we are supposed to say to the problem: Be lifted up and cast into the sea!)

Jesus said:

I assure you, most solemnly I tell you, if anyone steadfastly believes in Me, he will himself be able to do the things that I do; and he will do even greater things than these, because I go to the Father. And I will do [I Myself will grant] whatever you ask in My Name [as presenting all that I AM], so the Father may be glorified and extolled (through) the Son. Yes, I will grant [I Myself will do for you] whatever you shall ask in My Name [as presenting all that I AM].

John 14:12–14

We are supposed to go to God, boldly asking in faith for what we need, but we are to humble ourselves before Him and remind Him what His Word says. We must walk by faith, not by sight, because *it is the prayer of faith that God listens to*. You can have the desires of your heart if you have the faith to believe you receive them, but you have to believe first.

Here is an example of a specific prayer that I prayed: On a very cold, icy morning, when my son was still living at home and driving to college, I reminded him before he left home that there could be black ice so he needed to be very careful and leave room to stop safely. As he left home, I prayed that God would keep His mighty angels around my son's car and keep him and whoever rode with him safe from harm. The phone rang about thirty minutes later, and it was my son, who told me he had been in an accident but it wasn't his fault. He said a lady in a van stopped suddenly in front of him and he stopped okay behind her, but an eighteen-wheeler truck hadn't been able to stop and it hit his car in the rear and pushed it into the van ahead of him. Even though his car looked like an accordion in the front and the rear, the interesting and best part of this story is that my son had absolutely no injuries and the whole interior part of the car where people would sit was completely okay. (God does answer specific prayers, and He does keep His angels around us when we ask Him to.)

Here is another example of God answering specific prayers:

The transmission went out on my car and I didn't have much money and I didn't know anybody who could help me. I looked and looked for a reliable car that I could afford but couldn't find one. Then one night, in the middle of the night, I sat up in bed and I boldly prayed very specifically, asking God to help me find a reliable car that didn't cost very much. I didn't care how old it was as long as it was dependable because I had to go back and forth to work each day and I didn't have money to keep fixing it. I got a call early the next morning from a friend of the family who told me that he had been looking for a car for his teenage daughter and he found a creampuff of a car, he had already checked out, and he thought it would be perfect for me. He told me that the car was twelve years old but it had been sitting in a garage without being driven for about eleven of those years. He told me that the car was being sold for a small amount, the seller had put all new tires on it, there were only a few things that needed fixed and he would fix them for me, so the car would be as good as new. I knew that God had quickly and specifically answered my prayer, and I was able to get the car, which served me well for many years.

The Bible says that out of the mouth the heart speaks, so we must watch what we fill our minds and hearts with. We must not hold anger in our hearts, and we must never hold a grudge against anybody, because it will only hurt us. We are to forgive others no matter what they have done to us, and I know from experience how hard it is to forgive.

If we hold unforgiveness in our hearts against anyone, it blocks our blessings, healing, and every good thing coming to us from God. If our prayer request is according to God's Word, it is according to His will. God requires us to walk in the light of His Word, but if we don't believe His Word is true, we have no light. The Bible tells us that God's Word is a lamp unto our feet and a light unto our path. God gave us His Word to let us know what conditions must be met in order for us to receive these blessings and provisions.

When you pray, if you are holding anger and unforgiveness against somebody, please let go and let it drop, because unforgiveness blocks the blessings God has for you, so your prayers won't work. Sometimes you have to forgive the same person over and over again, seven times seventy times, as Jesus taught. That is why it is important not to let any anger or unforgiveness stay in your life.

Here is an example of how unforgiveness can block your blessings:

There was a time in my life when I was going through a very difficult time. For a while I felt like I was in a dark tunnel and God couldn't hear me anymore. I was complaining to a friend of mine about some very hurtful and awful things a person in my life had done to me, and she told me that I needed to forgive him for all the hurt he had caused my children and me and let it go. I told her I didn't think I could ever forgive him because he was still hurting us. She told me that the Bible says that unless we forgive those who have trespassed against us, God cannot forgive us. So after I read the Scriptures about unforgiveness in the Bible and prayed about it, I wrote a letter to this person and told him that I forgave him for what he had done to our children and me. I asked him to forgive me for anything I had done that hurt him. As soon as I sent that letter, it was as if I was out of the dark tunnel and the light shined in my life again.

As I read and studied the Bible, I could actually understand the Scriptures again. I truly learned how unforgiveness had been blocking the blessings God had for my children and me, but I also learned that sometimes you have to forgive the same person over and over again, as Jesus taught. That is why it is important not to let any anger or unforgiveness stay in your life. I learned to trust and lean on God for everything I needed or wanted for my family, and He took care of our needs.

When I tell people that I lean on God in every area of my life, they sometimes look at me like I'm crazy. Sometimes they say, "I believe God helps those who help themselves," as if I am not working and doing the things I should. I wonder if they really believe that God wants them to do everything by themselves, because I know that the more I lean on God, the more He blesses my children and me.

The Bible tells us:

> Let us all come forward and draw near with true (honest and sincere) hearts in unqualified assurance and absolute conviction engendered by faith (by that leaning of the entire human personality on God in absolute trust and confidence in His power, wisdom, and goodness), having our hearts sprinkled and purified from a guilty conscience and our bodies cleansed with pure water. So let us seize and hold fast and retain without wavering the hope we cherish and confess and our acknowledgment of it, for He who promised is reliable (sure) and faithful to His Word.
>
> Hebrews 10:22–23

God is a faith God, but without faith, it is impossible to please God. We are saved by faith and we are healed by faith (either your faith or somebody else's faith). Find Bible verses regarding God's provision for any problem or situation and claim them for yourself. You can build your faith by reading and studying these verses and speaking them out loud, standing firm in faith without doubting or wavering.

The answer to your problem or healing might be on the way to you, but if you speak doubt, it is stopped from reaching you. God laid our sickness on Jesus as He hung on the cross and Jesus took our infirmities and bore our sickness for us. Our healing has already been bought and paid for by Jesus, so we must claim our healing by faith, just like we claim our salvation by faith. We shouldn't just wait for God to do something about our problem, sickness, or pain; we must claim our healing in the Name of Jesus and continually believe that healing belongs to us. If we believe that Jesus died to take our sins, why can't we believe that Jesus died to take our sickness too? The Bible says He did.

Before Jesus ascended into heaven, He gave us the authority to use His Name, so we are supposed to go boldly to God and humbly ask for what we need or want from Him, in the Name of Jesus.

When we pray to God in the Name of Jesus, power is released from heaven in answer to our prayers. God's Word says to pray at all times in the spirit, in all manner of prayer. Jesus is the most powerful word in the world, and we have the authority to use it. Jesus gave us the power of attorney to use His Name against the devil. The key to this is to believe in the authority of Jesus' Name and the power of His Blood, praying and claiming what is ours through Jesus. We are not supposed to pray to Jesus; we are to pray to God in the Name of Jesus.

When we pray to God in the Name of Jesus, we should believe in our hearts that God is blessing us and answers to our prayers are on their way to us. We must have faith and praise God for answering our prayers even before we see the results, because God's Word tells us to "call things that be not as if they were." If we speak positively and believe and stand in faith, praising God and thanking Him for the answer to our prayer, even when we haven't seen it yet, God's Word says we will get what we prayed for.

We shouldn't blame God when our prayers are not answered if we have been speaking negatively or complaining and doubting, because these can stop our blessings from getting to us. And actually what we say out loud can become reality. Many times, we blame God for not answering our prayers, but in reality we might have been holding unforgiveness in our heart or doubted that we would be healed, which blocked our blessing from getting to us.

In the Scripture verses below, Jesus tells us to pray in His Name and much more:

> And when that time comes, you will ask nothing of me. I assure you, most solemnly I tell you, that My Father will grant you whatever you ask in My Name [as presenting all that I AM]. Up to this time you have not asked a [single] thing in My Name, but now ask and keep on asking and you will receive, so that your joy, (gladness, delight) may be full and complete. I have told you these things in parables (veiled language); the hour is now coming when I shall no longer speak to you in figures of speech, but I shall tell you about the Father in plain words and openly

(without reserve). At that time you will ask (pray) in My Name; and I am not saying that I will ask the Father on your behalf for it will be unnecessary. For the Father Himself (tenderly) loves you because you have loved Me and have believed that I came out from the Father. I came out from the Father, and have come into the world; again, I am leaving the world and going to the Father. I have told you these things, so that in Me you may have [perfect] peace and confidence. In the world you have tribulation and trials and distress and frustration, but be of good cheer [take courage; be confident, certain, undaunted]! For I have overcome the world. [I have deprived it of the power to harm you]!

John 16:23–28, 33

We are to find God's will in the Bible. It is God's will that we are saved through Jesus. It is God's will for us to be healed. It is God's will for our needs to be met. It is God's will for us to prosper and live in peace. It is God's will that we pray for others. It is God's will that the lost are saved. It is God's will for us to pray in Jesus' Name. It is God's will for us to use the Blood of Jesus against the devil. But we also must

understand that prayers will not work in an unforgiving heart. If we want our prayers to be answered,
we cannot hold a grudge or have an unforgiving
spirit. We cannot afford to have an unforgiving spirit
toward anyone, because it will hurt us spiritually and
steal our peace.

> You do not have, because you do not ask. [Or]
> you do ask [God for them] and yet fail to
> receive, because you ask with wrong purpose
> and selfish motives.
>
> James 4:2–3

God loves each of us, and He will accept us where
we are if we will let Him. When we believe in God
and receive Jesus as our Savior, then we must also ask
forgiveness for all the things that we have done that
hurt others. Nothing is too bad for God to forgive
us for, but we must also forgive all those who have
hurt us. If we are angry and unforgiving, we are in
darkness and our joy and blessings are blocked. We
cannot live in God's light and have His peace until
we forgive.

Your confession can be something like this:

In the Name of Jesus, I bind and rebuke sickness, weakness, disease, fear, poverty, impatience, anger, frustration, or anything that is not of God. I resist the devil in the Name of Jesus and the Word of my testimony. I refuse Satan a place in my family or in me, and he cannot take a place for himself because of the Blood of the Lamb that covers us. We run into Jesus' Name, which is a high tower, and we are safe by the authority of Jesus' Name and His Blood because God has given us the Blood and Name of Jesus to overcome Satan as we testify to its power.

Jesus encourages us to come together in prayer:

> Again I tell you, if two of you on earth agree about whatever (anything and everything) they may ask, it will come to pass and be done for them, by My Father in heaven. For wherever two or three are gathered (drawn together as My followers) in (into) My Name, there I AM in the midst of them.
>
> Matthew 18:19–20

Wherever two believers agree, God is right there with them. When we come together in His presence, planning, discussing, and praying. The group might be small, perhaps just two people, but if they agree on anything they ask, it shall be done. Every believer should find someone to join with him or her in prayer. God's Word says that when two agree in prayer, the power of the two increases tenfold over one. The Bible says that one shall put a thousand to flight but two will put ten thousand to flight. We can be mighty in prayer alone, but when we come together with other believers, what power our prayers have and miracles happen.

Many people pray "if it be your will," each time they pray, but that is not the way God wants us to pray. Jesus only prayed "If it be your will" once, and that was when He was asking God to take the cup from Him in the garden of Gethsemane, and Jesus knew that he was asking something that was not His Father's will. We are told to go boldly to His throne and humbly pray specific prayers for what we need or want. The only time we should pray "if it be your will" is when we don't know if it is His will.

It is important for us to remember that praise is just as important as our prayers are, in many ways, because when we are praising God, we get His attention. When sickness or other problems strike, we sometimes forget to praise God because celebration doesn't seem appropriate, but the Bible teaches us that praise and thanksgiving are very important to God. We praise because we are happy in good times, but when bad times come along, we sometimes forget what God has already done for us, and we stop praising Him. We should be praising God for even the smallest blessings that happen each day and for His past faithfulness in our life while we are awaiting His help.

When you are praying for healing or the answer to any problem and you have been waiting a long time for the answer, you probably are not praising and thanking God enough for all He has done and is doing for you. Try this: imagine an old-fashioned scale of justice with your prayers in one side of the scale and your praises in the other side of the scales. Are your prayers and praises equal? If your scale isn't as full on the praise side as it is on the prayer side, then you need to be praising and thanking God more. Remember, when you are praising God, you get His attention.

Jesus said:

Rejoice in the Lord always [delight, gladden yourselves in Him]; again I say, Rejoice! Do not fret or have any anxiety about anything, but in every circumstance and in everything, by prayer and petition (definite requests), with thanksgiving, continue to make your wants known to God. And God's peace [shall be yours, that tranquil state of a soul assured of its salvation through Christ, and so fearing nothing from God and being content with its earthly lot of whatever sort that is, that peace], which transcends all understanding, shall garrison and mount guard over your hearts and minds in Christ Jesus. For the rest, brethren, whatever is true, whatever is worthy of reverence and is honorable and seemly, whatever is just, whatever is pure, whatever is lovely and lovable, whatever is kind and winsome and gracious, if there is any virtue and excellence, if there is anything worthy of praise, think on and weigh and take account of these things [fix your mind on them]. Practice what you have learned and received and heard and seen in me, and model your way of living on it, and the God of peace (of untroubled, undisturbed well-being) will be with you.

Philippians 4:4, 6–9

God saw that there was no intercessor, so He sent Jesus to stand between God and us to plead our case. Believers are supposed to plead the cases of others and stand in the gap between them and plead their case through Jesus to God. We are also supposed to intercede for the lost because Jesus tells us to, the Great Commission. Sometimes we have an urge to pray when we don't even know whom it is we need to pray for. Others times, we can't get a friend or acquaintance out of our mind and we feel a burden or heaviness to pray. Sometimes it seems as though down deep within us there is an unexplainable sadness or uneasiness. The Spirit of God is trying to get you to intercede for some lost soul. God searches to find a believer who will intercede; you may not even know the person, but the Holy Spirit in you knows.

Sometimes people will ask us to pray for them or even someone who is a stranger to us and we don't know how to pray, but the Holy Spirit helps us make intercession for others. An intercessor is one who takes the place of or stands in the gap for another. The prayer of intercession is not for you, but you are interceding for another.

The Bible teaches that we need to pray out of our spirit and not just out of our heads. Spiritual praying is praying out of your spirit in Spirit-given utterances, and they can be utterances in your known language, or a tongue that is unknown to you. When we are praying intercessory prayers, we might not always understand the entire situation about which we are praying, but the Holy Spirit does. When we allow Him to help us in our prayer life, we will see amazing answers to our prayers. Every Spirit-filled believer can expect the Holy Spirit to help him pray in the Spirit. Speaking in tongues is not just an initial evidence of the Holy Spirit's indwelling; it is a continual experience for the rest of your life. Speaking in tongues will enrich your life spiritually, and it will enable you to help others and work with God on earth, through prayer.

Paul said:

> The Spirit Himself testifies together with our own spirit, [assuring us] that we are children of God. So the Holy Spirit comes to our aid and bears us up in our weakness; for we do not know what prayer to offer nor how to offer it

worthily as we ought, but the Spirit Himself goes to meet our supplication and pleads in our behalf with unspeakable yearnings and groanings too deep for utterance. And He Who searches the hearts of men knows what is in the mind of the [Holy] Spirit, because the Spirit intercedes and pleads [before God] in behalf of the saints (those who belong to God) according to and in harmony with God's will.

Romans 8:16, 26–27

We must stand in faith, trusting God's Word to work for us when we pray and claim what is ours by the authority of Jesus' Name and His Blood. If you are a believer, you are in Christ and you have authority over satanic forces. Jesus did that for you on the cross. If you are a believer, you must understand that Satan and his demon followers are defeated, dethroned, and stripped of their authority in your life, by Jesus. By Jesus' stripes, we were healed and made whole. Therefore, we need to claim, in the Name of Jesus, our healing and wholeness and the abundant life that belongs to us. We have the authority to take back what is rightfully ours from Satan if we have lost it. Speak the word. Claim what is yours. It works.

Find the Scripture that applies to your problem and claim what is yours as Jesus did when He said to the devil:

> Be gone, Satan! For it has been written, you shall worship the Lord your God and Him alone shall you serve.
>
> Matthew 4:10

One of my favorite Bible verses is:

> Little children, you are of God [you belong to Him] and have [already] defeated and overcome them [the agents of the antichrist], because He who lives in you is greater (mightier) than he who is in the world.
>
> 1 John 4:4

You can learn to trust and lean on God for everything you need or want, and He will take care of your needs. Believe in God, His Son, and The Holy Spirit; strengthen your faith and stand firm believing you will get what you pray for. You have direct access to God, through Jesus, and you can boldly go to God and humbly talk to Him and ask for help. Pray specifically for what you need or want, in the Name of Jesus, but never doubt that He will answer your prayers.

There are many people dying for lack of knowledge of God's Word, because they won't come close to Him and ask. Please don't lose out on what Jesus died to give you, draw near to Him and learn what is yours, ask and keep on asking.

Why Healing Belongs to Us

Some people blame God for their sickness or disease and say that it must be God's will for them to be sick, but sickness comes from Satan, not God. God wouldn't have sent Jesus to die on the cross to take our sin and sickness away and then keep putting sickness on us. God put our sicknesses on Jesus because He did not want us to keep bearing them. Jesus bore them so we all would be free. Healing belongs to us. God has provided it for us, but we have to possess it. We need to get into the Word of God and find out what belongs to us.

First Corinthians 15:26 tells us that physical death is an enemy of God, so sickness, disease, pain, infection, and even death are not from God but they are from Satan, who has *no authority* over those who belong to Jesus.

If something is promised to us in God's Word—it is God's will—and we need to claim it. We will not receive anything from God until we have the faith to believe that we will receive what we ask for. When we are praying for ourselves, our loved ones or an unbeliever, *it is our faith that gets our prayers answered.*

Sickness comes from the devil the same as sin does. God does not want us to be sick, so God laid our sicknesses and diseases on Jesus, and Jesus bore them. Jesus was stricken and afflicted with our sin, our sickness, our disease, and our infirmities. Therefore, Satan has no right or authority to put on us what Jesus already bore for us. God would not have had Jesus bear our sickness for us if He wanted us to be sick. The Bible says we were healed, so if we believe the Word of God, then we must believe that *Jesus took all our sickness the same as He took our sins and by His stripes we were healed.* The Word of God does not say that some of us were healed or that we might be healed; the Word of God says, "By His stripes we *were* healed." We can't pray that we will have no more trouble with the devil, but we can learn to take authority over him.

God has given us the Blood of Jesus and says it overcomes Satan as we testify to its power, which means that it will rob the devil of his power to harm us, but only if we stand firm in faith, believing that we are healed (or the problem is taken care of). We must plant our feet and stand firm in faith, resisting the devil, and standing on the Word of God, until our healing comes.

We are supposed to have faith constantly and resist the devil, even when our natural eyes tell us that we are still sick or the problem is still there, because in the Spirit, the healing (or answer to our problem) is on its way to us. We must have faith in our heart, believe what God's Word says, and confess with our mouths that we are healed by Jesus stripes and claim that healing.

We must have faith in what God has said in His Word and exercise our testimony against the devil in faith that this will cause the devil to flee from us. Having true faith means we believe that the devil and the disease (or problem) have gone, that healing (or the answer to the problem) takes place, and that we are well because the Blood of Jesus overcomes the devil and destroys his work.

According to God's Word, healing belongs to us just the same as salvation belongs to us. If we have received Jesus as our Savior, then we are saved from our sins and our healing has been paid for.

> Surely He has borne our griefs (sicknesses, weaknesses, and distresses) and carried away our sorrows and pains, yet we [ignorantly] considered Him stricken, smitten, and afflicted by God. But He was wounded for our transgressions, He was bruised for our guilt and iniquities; the chastisement [needful to obtain] peace and wellbeing for us was upon Him, and with the stripes [that wounded] Him we are healed and made whole.
>
> Isaiah 53:4–5

When we pray, we are supposed to believe that we are healed *before* the healing is evident. Everyone does not receive a miracle healing all at once. We must stand in faith, thanking and praising God for

His healing power that is at work in us until we see the healing manifested. This is true not only for healing but also in every other area of life. No matter what the need might be—material, spiritual, or financial—this is the way we receive.

> So be subject to God. Resist the devil [stand firm against him] and he will flee from you. Come close to God and He will come close to you.
>
> James 4:7–8

> Therefore humble yourselves [lower yourselves in your own estimation] under the mighty hand of God, that in due time He may exalt you, casting the whole of your care [all your anxieties, all your worries, all your concerns, once and for all] on Him, for He cares for you affectionately and cares about you watchfully. Be well balanced (temperate, sober of mind), be vigilant and cautious at all times; for the enemy of yours, the devil, roams around like a lion roaring [in fierce hunger], seeking someone to seize upon and devour. Withstand him; be firm in faith [against his onset, rooted, established, strong, immovable, and

determined], knowing that the same sufferings are appointed to your brotherhood (the whole body of Christians) throughout the world.

1 Peter 5:6–9

When Satan is trying to destroy our loved ones and us, we have the authority to plead the Blood of Jesus against the problem the devil has caused and claim our healing, protection, strength, prosperity, and other blessings, in the Name of Jesus. The faith that Jesus taught about is a spiritual faith that comes from your heart, not head faith. We need to have this spiritual faith for physical healing because we have all the emotions and the symptoms to deal with.

Prayer is successful only when it is based on the promises of God's Word. In the mind of God, we were already healed by Jesus' stripes, so we need to claim our healing in the Name of Jesus. It is not a matter of God's healing an individual; it is a matter of the individual accepting the gift God already has provided. We need to claim our healing in the Name of Jesus and stand firm in faith that we are healed, even when we can't see our healing in the natural yet.

> My people are destroyed for lack of knowledge; because you have rejected knowledge, I will also reject you that you shall be no priest to Me; seeing you have forgotten the law of your God, I will also forget your children.
>
> Hosea 4:6

We need to take this literally. This means people are dying for lack of knowledge of God, His Son, and His Word. God gives us His Word to let us know what conditions must be met in order for us to receive these blessings and provisions. God has His part to play; but man also has His part to play, and there are conditions that have to be met by us. We must ask and have enough faith to believe that healing belongs to us. We must receive it in faith the same way we did with salvation. God laid our sickness on Jesus, who took our infirmities and bore our sickness, so the provision has already been made. Your healing has already been bought and paid for, so you need to claim it in the Name of Jesus.

Get into the New Testament and read and study and find out what belongs to you. If it is promised to you, if the Bible says it's yours, it's provided for you. You must possess it through faith. Find the Bible verses regarding God's provision of healing and claim them for yourself.

Mark 11:22–26 tells us what we need to do to get our prayers answered:

1) *"Have faith in God constantly."* (This shows that faith is very important.)

2) *"Whoever says to this mountain, be lifted up and thrown into the sea!"* (This does not mean a real mountain … it means whatever problem you're dealing with (sickness, healing, pain, finances, etc.) Here is an example of how we are supposed to speak to the problem: You are to say: In the Name of Jesus, I bind you Satan and I press the Blood of Jesus against the sickness and you must flee from me. Get thee behind me, Satan! I claim in the Name of Jesus that I am healed by Jesus' stripes.)

3) *"And does not doubt in his heart but believes that what he says will take place, it will be done for him. For this reason I am telling you, whatever you ask for in prayer, believe (trust and be confident) that it is granted to you, and you will get it."* You can say: I stand firm in faith that I am healed from the top of my head to

the bottom of my feet and I believe that I am healed by Jesus' stripes. Thank you, Jesus!

4) *"And whenever you stand praying, if you have anything against anyone, forgive him and let it drop ... but if you do not forgive neither will your Father in heaven forgive your failings and shortcomings."* (This is not a suggestion ... this is what the Bible scripture is telling you to do.) You must truly forgive (in your heart) everybody you are angry with. You can say: I Forgive everyone that I have been angry with (names) and I let it drop. (Then thank and praise God and believe that the answer to your prayer is already on its way to you.)

You should pray using these principles for any need or healing or any problem you have, because Jesus told us to pray this way. Jesus is not talking about moving a mountain; He is talking about moving your sickness (or problem)—whatever is in your way. If you use these four principles in any prayer and you stand firm in faith that God is now answering your prayer, *Jesus said it will be done for you.*

You can build your faith by reading and studying these verses and speaking them out loud while standing firm in faith without doubting or wavering. Your healing might have been on the way to you, but your doubt or negativity stopped it from reaching you.

This is the confidence we should have in God. If we ask anything according to His will, He hears us, and if we know that He hears us, then we should start praising him and thanking Him for the answer to our prayer even before we see the manifestation with our natural eyes.

A sample prayer would be:

> Dear God, Your Word says, "By Jesus' stripes I am healed," so I claim the healing Jesus died to give me and I stand firm in faith that I am healed. I believe the Word of God, and according to the Word of God, I am healed. I am not trying to get healed. I don't have to get it because Jesus has already gotten my healing for me, so it belongs to me. In the name of Jesus, I claim the healing that belongs to me according to the Word of God. I plead the Blood of Jesus over and around and through my body because God's Word says the Blood of Jesus overcomes the devil and he must flee from me. In the Name of Jesus, I command you, Satan, to flee from me and take the

sickness, pain, weakness, (name the symptoms
if you want to) with you now! Amen Thank
you Jesus! Healing belongs to me! Praise God!
(Now stand firm believing you are healed.)

The Bible tells us to offer the sacrifice of praise
to God, so even if you don't see results to your prayer
yet, keep praising God for what He has already done
in your life and believe that you are healed.

The devil is constantly trying to get us to lose our
faith and our peace, so he is constantly putting aches
and pains on us, but the Bible clearly states that Jesus
came to take our sins and sickness from us, so we can
know without a doubt that God wants us healed and
stand firm in faith believing our healing is on its way
to us.

I have heard some people say they think God is
punishing them, but according to the New Testament
Covenant, if you are a believer, God remembers your
sins no more. God does not remember that you
have ever done anything wrong because your sins
are washed away. When we come in faith according
to God's Word, God will make His Word good if
we stand on it. God's Word teaches us that God's

ways are not our ways, so we don't have to understand everything but have faith in God's Word and do what it tells us to do.

> For My thoughts are not your thoughts, neither are your ways My ways, says the Lord. For as the heavens are higher than the earth, so are My ways higher than your ways, and My thoughts higher than your thoughts. For as the rain and snow come down from heaven, and returns not there again, but water the earth and make it bring forth and sprout, that it may give seed to the sower and bread to the eater. So shall My Word be that goes forth out of My mouth; it shall not return to Me void [without producing any effect, useless], but it shall accomplish that which I please and purpose, and it shall prosper in the thing for which I sent it.
>
> Isaiah 55:8–11

Practically all the prayers of the Old Testament are prayers of covenant men; Abraham, Joshua, Elijah, David, and Moses all had covenants with God. God gave heed to their petitions, and their prayers were answered. The believer today has a better covenant established upon better promises. *God redeemed mankind through Jesus Christ and authority was restored to believers through Jesus.* God is not playing Superman in the world. He has given mankind free will, and God will not force His way on us. We must draw near to Him and believe that He is God and Jesus is His Son, forgive and ask.

When we pray, we are joining forces with God the Father, fellowshipping with Him, and carrying out His will upon the earth. God will do nothing for humanity unless someone asks Him to do it. We limit God by the lack of prayer in our life. God is waiting for you to come to Him and ask Him for help. God has given believers the authority to claim what is ours according to God's Word and ask for protection and whatever help we need, but God will do nothing unless someone asks Him to.

I believe we have more authority than we realize we have on the earth. God said, "Let us plead together." I believe that we sometimes limit God with our prayer life. We are supposed to go boldly to God and humbly pray, putting Him in remembrance of His Word, and plead our case for what the Bible says is ours; always praying in Jesus' Name.

Different Kinds of Prayers

We are supposed to go boldly to the throne of God and humbly pray specific prayers; then praise God for the results even before we see the results in the natural. There may be times that you won't get results from your prayers and you may never understand why, but don't blame God. We can't always understand God's reasons or what is happening in the spiritual realm, but if you stay close to God, your prayer life will be good. Also, remember that over time our bodies eventually will wear out and each of us will die (unless you are lucky enough to go in the rapture before then), but don't stop praying for healing or relief from pain even when you are older. Never doubt that God loves you, hears your prayers, and wants you to talk to Him and even plead with Him and remind Him of His Word. If you are praying an intercessory prayer for somebody else, remember God won't go against that person's wishes.

If you have trouble getting results from your prayers, maybe you should look at what could be blocking your blessings:

- Are you holding unforgiveness against someone?

- Do you doubt God wants you healed?

- Are you standing firm in faith, or are you wavering in your faith?

- Are you speaking negative words about your situation?

- Does what you asked for in prayer go against God's Word?

- Have you forgotten to thank and praise God for things He has done in the past?

- Are you doing things in your life that you know you aren't supposed to be doing?

Jesus gives us an example of how to pray in the prayer in Matthew 6:9, which we call the Lord's Prayer:

> Our Father which art in heaven, Hallowed be thy name. Thy kingdom come. Thy will be done in earth, as it is in heaven. Give us this day our daily bread. And forgive us our trespasses, as we forgive those who trespass against us. And lead us not into temptation, but deliver us from evil; for thine is the kingdom, and the power, and the glory, forever. Amen
>
> Matthew 6:9-13, KJV

Here are examples of prayers for healing that you can personalize for your own use or change to meet your needs. For example: Fill in the blank lines with the name of the person you are praying for and other lines are for you to name whatever the problem is: name the disease, sickness, pain, weakness, and other health problems.

> I overcome the devil by the Blood of the Lamb and the Word of my testimony; so in the Name of Jesus, I bind and rebuke _____ (specific problem) that has

attacked me and I cast it into the sea! And in the Name of Jesus, I plead the Blood of Jesus against _____ (specific problem), and I render it harmless and ineffective against me. So, Satan, you must leave now and take _____ (specific problem) with you. In the Name of Jesus, I claim healing in every cell, tissue, organ, muscle, and every part of my body. In the Name of Jesus, I forbid any disease, weakness, virus, infection, or any malfunction in my body and I claim I will not die but live the fulfillment of my days in good health. I pray in the Name of Jesus. Amen. I praise you and thank you for the healing!

Dear God, I pray in Jesus' Name, and I rest upon Your Word that Jesus Himself took our infirmities and bore our sicknesses and by His stripes we were healed. The Word says that Christ redeemed us from the curse of the law as he hung on the cross and Jesus has set us free. Father, Your Word says, These signs shall follow them that believe, in My Name, they shall lay hands on the sick and they shall recover and have the fulfillment of their days, so I am pleading for that because (name)

_____ is too young to die, and he/she is one of your saints and is needed by his/her family and friends. In the Name of Jesus, I lay my hand on (name) _____ and I claim the healing that Jesus died to give us. I ask you to manifest your healing because, Lord, your Word says that the prayer of faith shall save the sick. Matthew 16:19 tells us that Jesus said, "I give you the keys to the kingdom, whatever you bind on earth will be bound in heaven, whatever you loose on earth will be loosed in heaven." So I pray in the Name of Jesus, and I rebuke the pain, sickness, and even death; I command it to leave in the Name of Jesus. Father, I believe Thy Word is true so in Jesus Name, I claim the complete and total healing of (name) _____ from the top of his/her head to the bottom of his/her feet. I thank you and praise you for this healing! Amen

I overcome the devil by the Blood of the Lamb and the Word of my testimony; so in the Name of Jesus, I bind and rebuke _____ (specific problem) that has attacked me and I cast it into the sea. And in the Name of Jesus, I plead the Blood of Jesus against _____ (specific problem), and render it harmless and ineffective against me. So, in the Name of Jesus—Satan, you must leave now, and take _____ (specific problem) with you. In the Name of Jesus, I claim healing in every cell, tissue, organ, muscle, and every part of my body. In the Name of Jesus, I forbid any disease, weakness, virus, infection, or any malfunction in my body and I claim I will not die but live the fulfillment of my days in good health. I pray in the Name of Jesus. Amen.

I am a believer and I overcome the world, the flesh, and the devil by the Blood of the Lamb and the Word of my testimony. In the Name of Jesus, I cast out demons, I speak with new tongues, I lay hands on the sick and they do recover. So, in the Name of Jesus, I lay hands on _____ and I ask for God's healing power to flow through _____ to every organ, muscle, cell, tissue, and every part of her/his body to heal _____ body from the top of her/his head to the bottom of her/his feet so her/his body will function in the perfection to which God created it to function. In the Name of Christ Jesus, I pray and I believe in faith that _____ is physically, mentally, and emotionally healed and made strong, healthy, and whole by the healing Blood of Jesus and the power of the Holy Spirit of God. I claim in the Name of Jesus that _____ is healed and I stand believing in agreement with others that _____ is completely healed from the top of her/his head to the bottom of her/his feet. We will not waver in our faith because we believe the Word of God, which clearly says that we can have whatever we say in the Name of Jesus. Amen

I overcome the devil by the Blood of the Lamb and the Word of my testimony; so in the Name of the Lord, Jesus Christ, I bind and rebuke the _____ (specific problem) that has attacked _____ (name) and I cast it into the sea. And in the Name of Jesus, I plead the Blood of Jesus against _____ (specific problem), and render it harmless and ineffective against _____ so, Satan, you must leave now and take _____ (specific problem) with you. In the Name of Jesus, I claim healing in every cell, tissue, organ, muscle, and every part of my/her/his body. In the Name of Jesus, I forbid any disease, weakness, virus, infection, or any malfunction in my/her/his body and I claim _____ will not die but live the fulfillment of my/her/his days in good health. I pray in Jesus' Name. Amen. I praise you and thank you for this healing!

We are supposed to come boldly to the throne of God and humbly pray specific prayers for what we need or for the answer to whatever problem we have and put God in remembrance of His Word. He encourages us to plead together with Him and humbly declare why we believe our pleading will be proved right.

God can meet every need we have, so plead your case with God. Talk to Him as the loving Father that He is. Tell Him what is troubling you, and if you are at your wits' end, just lift yourself up to Him and ask Him to take care of the problem because you can't do any more. This doesn't mean that you stop work and do nothing for yourself; this means that you do everything you can to solve the problem, with the help of Jesus.

I have read many testimonies of different people that have actually died and gone to heaven, but people were praying for them and pleading with God for their recovery, and Jesus sent them back to earth, even though they wanted to stay in heaven. That shows us how powerful our prayers are with God. He listens to the pleadings of His children and wants to please them. It is so comforting to know that you can plead with God and He will hear your prayers and your pleas. I believe we have more authority with God than we know or have ever used upon the earth.

I believe that we have limited God with our prayer life. We limit God when we don't pray or when our faith wavers after we have prayed or we doubt the healing will happen. We must keep our faith strong and believe in the *supernatural love and power of God*, because as long as we are praying in faith and not doubting, God's angels are fighting the devil for the healing of the person we are praying for. We need to ask and keep on asking, and even plead with God when something is important to us, especially healing, because Jesus died to set us free and He won our healing at the cross.

We are supposed to plead the Blood of Jesus over and around our loved ones, and against the devil and he must leave. Jesus told His disciples to pray in His Name when He went to be with His Father in heaven, so we are supposed to pray that way now. Jesus taught that we should be persistent in our prayers and keep asking and seeking and knocking and Jesus will open the door.

Example of a prayer for loved ones and yourself:

Dear heavenly Father, I thank You for all that You have done and are doing for my children, grandchildren, our loved ones, and me. I pray in Jesus' name, and I lift up the shield of faith and the protective Blood of Jesus over and around each of us. Please keep us safe, healthy, strong, and well. Make a hedge of your mighty angels around each of us and fight our battles with the devil for us. Please strengthen our inner man each day and open the eyes of our hearts and flood us with your godly wisdom, discernment, and the knowledge of you. Send labors to those who need it, and take the scales from their eyes and ears and prepare their hearts to hear your words. Please keep us in your safe embrace and guard our hearts, minds, and bodies from evil. Please bless us, prosper us, strengthen us, and heal us in every area of our lives: spiritually, physically, mentally, emotionally, socially, and financially. I pray in the Name of Jesus. Amen.

Before Jesus left the earth, He gave the right of intercession to His followers, and that means us. Jesus gave believers His power of attorney to claim and expect that His Father would hear and answer prayers asked in Jesus' Name. What Jesus taught was not just for His disciples; His teachings were also for us today. God is waiting for each of us to get into His Word and find out what belongs to us. If the Bible says it's ours, if it is promised to us, it is provided for each of us, but we must possess it through faith.

Intercessory prayers are the prayers offered for others as we stand between others and God and we plead on their behalf. The Bible tells us to pray for our nation and those in authority.

Here is a prayer that I pray for our nation:

Dear Father, I come to You in the Name of Jesus, thanking You and praising You for our great nation and the plan You gave to our forefathers by which to govern our nation. The Bible tells us to pray for those in authority, so I lift up the president of the United States to You and I pray that You would give our leader discernment, understanding, and knowledge in every decision he makes for our nation daily. I pray that he will not follow his own preferences and his agenda, but be governed by Your principles and the Constitution of the United States. Please surround him with men and women of integrity who place God and the good of the United States above their own preferences and agendas. I pray for the Congress of the United States of America, both the House of Representatives and the Senate, and the Supreme Court justices and all lawmakers in the United States of America; I pray that You would convict our legislative body to make laws that are motivated by Your hand rather than their own selfish preferences to strengthen and prosper our nation. I pray that godly judges would be elected and appointed to our judicial system and they will make rulings in line with Your will. I pray that You would raise up men and women who are guided by Your hand to be elected to every position of authority in our nation. Father, please help us to elect godly people each election and defeat those who have been pushing their own agenda on the American citizens for many years in our government. I pray that You would convict Christians in their hearts to stand up and be counted on important issues and for the spiritual influence in our nation. I pray that Christians will not only stand up and speak up, but that their prayers and service will affect the spiritual complexion of our entire nation and influence our politics, economy, media, and our entire society. I pray that You would make a hedge around our nation and surround us with Your mighty protective angels. I pray that You will grant our leaders, FBI, CIA, Homeland Security, immigration authorities, the port authority, the Coast Guard, policemen, firemen, military men and women, and other first responders with wisdom and discernment at all times for the peace and safety of our nation, and may they escape death and injury while protecting others. I know that Israel is special to you, so I pray for the peace and protection of Israel, the United States, our allies, and all peaceful people of the world.

Important things to remember when you pray:

- Remember: God is your loving Father. It is Satan who wants to harm you.

- Faith is essential to get your prayers answered.

- Believe that the answer to your prayer is on its way to you when you pray.

- The Blood of Jesus and the Name of Jesus are powerful against Satan.

- Stand firm in faith because you should never doubt or waiver when you pray.

- Unforgiveness will keep your blessings from getting to you from God.

- Praise and thank God for all that He has done and is doing for you.

Our Words are Powerful

God created the universe by His words. We are created in the image of God, so we are supposed to release our faith in words. Man is a physical, mental, and spiritual being. The Word of God conceived in our human spirit and spoken out of our mouth becomes creative power that works for us. Jesus told us to attend to His words, for they are life and health to all our flesh. God's Word is full of power, but His Word is powerless when left unspoken.

Every spiritual law and faith principle that God set forth in His Word was for our benefit. We can have what we say when we learn to release faith from the heart in our words. As we begin to speak the Word of God from our heart, our faith mixed with God's Word will produce peace, prosperity, health, and healing because God's Word said it would. We should train ourselves to speak God's Word and use God's Word to defeat Satan as Jesus did.

When we believe and confess the Word of God, it strengthens us and grows our faith. We need to believe in our heart that God's Word is powerful, and we must speak His Word in faith and praise and give thanks to God for the positive results even before we see the results in the natural. We need to speak God's Word, stand firm in faith, and believe with our hearts that even though we cannot see the results in the natural yet, they are on their way in the spirit.

God's Word says:

> Do not be conformed to this world (this age), (fashioned after and adapted to its external, superficial customs), but be transformed (changed) by the renewal of your mind (by its new ideals and its new attitude), that you may prove (for yourselves) what is the good and acceptable and perfect, will of God, even

the thing which is good and acceptable and
perfect (in His sight for you).

Romans 12:2

The Lord says:

For My thoughts are not your thoughts,
neither are your ways My ways. For as the
heavens are higher than the earth, so are My
ways higher than your ways, and My thoughts
than your thoughts. For as the rain and snow
come down from the heavens, and return not
there again, but water the earth and makes it
bring forth and sprout, that it may give seed to
the sower and bread to the eater. So shall My
Word be that goes forth out of My mouth:
it shall not return to Me void, [without
producing any effect, useless], but it shall
accomplish that which I please and purpose,
and it shall prosper in the thing for which I
sent it.

Isaiah 55:8–11

The body of Christ must understand the authority we have through Jesus and begin to live in that
authority. Believers must read and study God's Word

for their faith to grow. We must speak the Word of God about things *that be not as though they are* and confess victory in the face of apparent defeat, confess abundance in the face of apparent lack, and confess healing and health in the face of sickness.

Christianity is sometimes called the great confession, but most Christians who are defeated in life are defeated because they believe the wrong thing. Proverbs 6:2 says, "You are snared with the words of your lips, you are caught by the speech of your mouth." Spoken words program your spirit heart either for success or defeat.

As we begin to speak the Word of God from our heart, our faith mixed with God's Word will produce peace, prosperity, health, and healing, because God's Word said it would. We need to believe in our heart that God's Word is powerful. We need to speak God's Word, stand firm in faith, and believe with our hearts that even though we cannot see the results in the natural yet, they are on their way in the spirit. We must praise and give thanks to God for positive results even before we see the results in the natural.

We need to watch what we are saying and bringing into our lives, because our constant complaining and saying negative things about ourselves and our children, can become a reality. Our words are powerful and can become a reality, so we must definitely watch what we say.

> So shall My Word be that goes forth out of My mouth; it shall not return to Me void, [without producing any effect, useless], but it shall accomplish that which I please and purpose, and it shall prosper in the thing for which I sent it.
>
> Isaiah 55:11

Here are some examples of what you should be confessing to fit a need or the problem in your life:

- I have faith in God constantly. I say unto this (problem), "Be thou removed, (problem) and be cast into the sea!" I do not doubt in my heart, but I believe those things that I say will come to pass and I will have whatever I say.

- Jesus gave me the authority to use His Name. That which I bind on earth is bound in heaven, and that which I loose on earth is loosed in heaven. Therefore, in the name of the Lord, Jesus Christ, I bind and cast down the principalities and powers of the darkness of this world and spiritual wickedness in high and low places; and in Jesus' Name, I render them harmless and ineffective against me.

- I am a believer, and these signs do follow me. In the name of Jesus, I cast out demons, I speak with new tongues, and I lay hands on the sick and they do recover.

- I will not let the Word of God depart from before my eyes, for it is life, health, and healing to all my flesh.

- No man shall take me out of God's hands, for I have eternal life.

- I let the peace of God rule in my heart, and I refuse to worry about anything.

- God is on my side. God is in me now, so who can be against me?

- I believe and accept whatever God's Word says, and I put it into practice.

- I am redeemed from spiritual death and the curse of the Law. I am redeemed from poverty, I am redeemed from sickness, and from spiritual death. For poverty He has given me wealth; for weakness He has given me strength; for sickness He has given me good health; for death He has given me eternal life.

- I am not conformed to this world, but I am transformed by the renewing of my mind.

- I am of God and have overcome Satan and the world by the Blood of the Lamb and the Word of my testimony; for greater is the Holy Spirit in me than the devil that is in the world.

- I will fear no evil for thou art with me Lord, your Word and your Spirit they comfort me.

- No weapon formed against me shall prosper, for my righteousness is of the Lord. Whatever I do will prosper for I am like a tree that is planted by the rivers of water.

- I take the shield of faith and the Word of my testimony, and I quench every fiery dart that the wicked one brings against me.

- I am submitted to God and the devil flees from me because I resist him in the Name of Jesus.

- Great is the peace of my children and grandchildren for they are taught of the Lord.

- I have no lack for my God supplies all of my needs according to His riches in glory.

- The Lord has pleasure in the prosperity of His servant, and Abraham's blessings are mine.

- I delight myself in the Lord and He gives me the desires of my heart.

- I trust in the Lord with all my heart and I lean not on my own understanding; in all my ways I acknowledge Him and He directs my path.

- The joy of the Lord is my strength, so the Lord is the strength of my life.

- I am strengthened with all might according to God's glorious power, so I will do all things through Christ who strengthens me.

- I let the peace of God rule in my heart and I refuse to worry about anything.

- I will not let the Word of God depart from before my eyes for it is life to me; I have found it and it is health and healing to all my flesh.

The confession of God's Word calls for healing, which is already ours, but is not manifested in our bodies. It takes time for us to renew our mind and develop faith in God's Word, but the things we continue to confess daily eventually become a part of us, but it doesn't happen overnight. Confessing God's Word helps grow your faith to the point where it will seem natural for you to receive healing, or answer to other problems, through the Word of God. Take the time now to develop your faith, so if you have a life or death situation you will know without a doubt what to do.

Here are some Scriptures you can confess over specific illnesses and health problems; change them to fit whatever healing or health problem you have:

- I am free from unforgiveness and strife.

- I forgive others as Christ has forgiven me.

- God's love has been poured out in my heart through the Holy Spirit.

- I attend to God's Words and I will not let them depart from before my eyes. I keep them in the midst of my heart, for they are life, strength, and healing to all my flesh.

- Jesus personally bore my sins, sickness, weakness, and pain in His body on the cross; therefore I claim that I am healed by Jesus' stripes. I give no place to sickness, weakness, viruses, infection, inflammation, disease or pain, because God sent His Word and healed me.

- I am an overcomer. I overcome the world, the flesh and the devil, by the Blood of the Lamb and the word of my testimony.

- Dear God, you have given me abundant life. I receive that life through Your Word and it flows to every organ, cell and tissue of my body bringing strength, healing, good health, and the fulfillment of my days.

- No evil will befall me, neither shall any plague come near my dwelling, because God has given His angels charge over me and they keep me in all my ways. In my pathway is life, strength, healing, good health, and peace in every area of my life:

spiritually, mentally, physically, emotionally, socially, and financially.

- That which God has not planted in me is dissolved and rooted out of my body, in the Name of Jesus. This strength, healing, and good health is engrafted into every fiber of my being and I am alive with the life of God.

- Every organ, cell, tissue, and every part of my body and mind, function in the perfection that God created them to function. In the Name of Jesus, I forbid any sickness, disease, pain, weakness, or any malfunction in my body or mind.

- Father, Your Word is manifest in my body causing all malfunctions to disappear. I make a demand on my muscles, bones, and joints to be strong and function properly, in the Name of Jesus.

- Father, Your Word has become a part of me. It is flowing in my bloodstream. It is flowing to every organ, cell and tissue of my body, restoring and transforming my body.

- I have a strong healthy heart and every heartbeat floods my body with life and cleanses me of disease and pain.

- The life of God flows in my blood and cleanses my arteries of all matter that does not pertain to life. My blood pressure, cholesterol, and blood sugar are perfect.

- My heartbeat is normal and it beats with the rhythm of life, carrying the life of God throughout my body.

- In the name of Jesus, I forbid my body to be deceived in any manner. Body, you will not be deceived by any infection, virus or disease germ; you will not work against life or good health in any way. Every cell of my body supports good health, strength, and life.

- My mind, body, and immune system grow stronger every day. In the name of Jesus, I speak life to my mind, body, and immune system and I forbid confusion in them. The same Spirit that raised Christ from the grave dwells in me and quickens my mind, body, and immune system with the life and wisdom of God, which guards the life and health of my body.

- Body, I speak the Word of God to you and in the Name of Jesus, I claim complete and total healing from the top of my head to the bottom of my feet and a long healthy life and the fulfillment of my years.

Confessing the Word of God can change your world, because it can change an image of sickness into an image of healing and good health. When you continue to speak God's Word it will strengthen your spirit and your faith will grow. Confess the Word with authority over your body at least 2 or 3 times a day. When you confess God's Word, His medicine will be life and good health to your mind and body.

Believers Have
Authority Over Satan

There is a Spirit world beyond our human eyes and if we could see into it, we would see Satan and his demons causing sickness, pain, disease, destruction, and the death that is in this world. We would also see God's mighty warrior angels fighting battles against the devil and his evil spirits for those who have accepted God's grace and received Jesus as their Savior.

Earth is Satan's territory, so the whole world around us is under the power of the evil one. Believers are in the world, but they are not of the world; they are children of light, not darkness. It is not God who withholds answers to our prayers. God sends the answer the minute we pray, but there are forces out in the heavens fighting to intercept these answers and keep them from getting to us. That is why it is so important for us to stand firmly in faith, believing that our prayers are answered, and never doubt or waver in our faith.

The Bible teaches:

> For though we walk (live) in the flesh, we are not carrying on our warfare according to the flesh and using mere human weapons. For the weapons of our warfare are not physical [weapons of flesh and blood]; but they are mighty before God, for the over-throw and destruction of strongholds.
>
> 2 Corinthians 10:3–4

The Bible tells us that when Satan is finally eliminated from the earth, there will be nothing that hurts or destroys. That will be a great day, but we do not have to let Satan dominate us now. Even though Satan is the ruler of this world, he does not have a right to dominate us as believers. But as long as we are in this world, Satan will still try to kill and destroy us.

Believers are under the authority of Jesus, and the devil knows it, but he will continue to try to draw us away from God and His protection and blessings. We must remember that even though Satan will continue to attack us, we need to call on Jesus and know that when we speak the Name of Jesus and plead His Blood against the devil, the devil must flee.

Paul tells us:

> Be strong in the Lord [be empowered through your union with Him]; draw your strength from Him [that strength which His boundless might provides]. Put on God's whole armor [the armor of a heavy-armed soldier which God supplies], that you may be able successfully to stand up against [all] the strategies and the deceits of the devil. For we are not wrestling with flesh and blood [contending only with physical opponents], but against the despotisms, against the powers, against [the master spirits who are] the world rulers of this present darkness, against the spirit forces of wickedness in the heavenly (supernatural) sphere. Therefore,

put on God's complete armor, that you may be able to resist and stand your ground on the evil day [of danger], and having done all [the crisis demands], to stand [firmly in your place].

Ephesians 6:10–13

Jesus tells His disciples about the power (He has given them) over the devil and his evil forces, and this power is for believers today:

Behold, I give unto you power to tread on serpents and scorpions, and [physical and mental strength and ability] over all the power that the enemy [possesses]; and nothing shall by any means harm you.

Luke 10:19

Prayer is a powerful thing. If we belong to God, He hears our prayers and immediately releases His power for answers to our prayers. When we pray for other people, even when they are unbelievers, the power of God is released through our prayers of intercession. When we have accepted Jesus as our

Savior, we have accepted His free grace and everlasting life, so we also need to accept His rules.

The Word of God is the only moral absolute. Where our mind goes, our actions are going to follow. Jesus can heal us everywhere we hurt, and He wants us to have a joyful, peaceful, prosperous life. But it is ultimately our choice, and we have a part to play. We need to remember that even though Satan will continue to attack us, we need only speak the Name of Jesus and plead His Blood against the devil. The devil must flee.

When we are young, we learn Bible verses and learn to pray, but as we get older, we sometimes stop praying and let the world influence us. We start making bad choices and we blame God for our misfortune and wonder why God would let bad things happen us. God is not the one we should be blaming for our troubles because God does not cause bad things to happen to our loved ones and us.

The Bible scripture below tells us that God sends His angels to protect believers:

The Angel of the Lord encamps around those who fear Him [who revere and worship Him with awe] and each of them He delivers.

Psalm 34:7

The name of the Lord is a strong tower; the righteous man [upright and in right standing with God] runs into it and is safe, high [above evil] and strong.

Proverbs 18:10

The Bible says that Jesus healed the sick and rebuked the storms, so this tells us that God doesn't cause sickness, storms, and the other catastrophes that happen on earth, because if God caused the storms, then Jesus would not have rebuked them. Jesus said, "For I have come down from heaven not to do My own will and purposes but to do the will and purpose of Him Who sent Me" (John 6:38). All the healings, all the miracles, all the works that Jesus did, God did through Jesus. God was the Holy Spirit in Jesus when He walked on earth, and God is the Holy Spirit in those of us who believe in Him and receive His Son, Jesus, as their Savior.

Our protection, deliverance, and safety lie in knowing how to overcome the devil. Our whole being; spirit, soul, and body, has been redeemed, bought away from Satan's power at a great cost. God has given us the Blood of Jesus and says it overcomes Satan as we testify to its power; when we plead it against the devil, he must flee from us.

We wonder why we have all these storms, floods, and other weather catastrophes and we blame God when, in reality, we humans keep messing with God's creation, along with the help of the devil. Satan still roams the earth, looking for whomever he may destroy, and he causes the storms, floods, destruction, and sickness and death, not God.

God gave us eternal life, through His Son, so we have confidence in Jesus. We are sure that if we ask anything according to His will, He listens to and hears us. We know positively that we are of God and the world around us is under the power of Satan. Man is not just a physical and mental man, but he is also a spiritual being. We should not be conformed to this world, but be changed by the renewal of our minds. For whatever is born of God is victorious over the world, and this is the victory of faith that conquers the world. He who believes that Jesus is the Son of God and who adheres to, trusts in, and relies on that fact, is victorious over the world.

When Satan attacks us in spirit, soul, or body, we must quickly meet him with: the Name of Jesus, our word of faith testimony, and the powerful Blood of Jesus, which God said overcomes Satan and he must flee. We must truly believe that Satan and his word are now overcome and that they do flee, even though we see and feel no change. Remember, faith is the evidence of things not seen, and we are to call those things that be not, as if they were. We must believe that the devil and the disease have gone, healing takes their place, and we are well, because the Blood of Jesus overcomes the devil and destroys his work. (This doesn't just work for healing; you can use it against any problem the devil puts in your way.)

Sometimes faith is tried by a return of the old symptoms of pain and disease; they come back just as they were before the healing. The Bible tells us that Satan will say, "I will go back to the place from whence I came out"; but if the Blood and faith are there, he has to leave. Then you must plead the Blood of Jesus, speak your testimony (according to God's

Word), and declare that God has healed you and that Satan cannot put the disease back because you resist Him steadfastly in faith, without doubt, fear, or wavering, but believing it will be done for you.

Christians have authority over Satan that Jesus gave to us. Faith in the Blood of Jesus, the Name of Jesus, and what God has said in His Word, when exercised in testimony against the devil, will cause him to flee from us. Jesus has already died once, and He shed His Blood to save and heal all of us, so He has already done everything He needs to do to provide our redemption from our sins and sickness. That which the Lord has legally purchased and provided for us becomes ours when we believe the Word of God in our hearts, confess with our mouths that it is true, and claim that it is ours. We must claim what is already ours in Christ Jesus.

The Bible says that no weapons formed against us shall prosper if we belong to Jesus and learn to use the weapons He has provided us for protection. We need to stay under the covering of prayer and lift up the shield of faith and the protective Blood of Jesus over our loved ones and us. The Blood of Jesus overcomes the devil and he must flee, so we need to stand firm in God's Word, because all the weapons we need for help against the evil in this world are at our disposal and we must learn to use them.

We are told not to be afraid and not to worry or be anxious for anything, but to constantly have faith that God will take care of our every need when we belong to Jesus. We must also remember that God sends His angels to protect us and encamp around us when we ask God for His protection.

Our words can be a blessing to us and they can also be a curse to us. We must watch what we are saying and bringing into our lives, because our words can bring us blessings, but they can also hurt us. When we are constantly complaining and saying negative things, our words can become reality, so we must definitely watch what we say.

Faith is the key to trusting in the Lord and establishing your heart on God's Word. It is not pleasing to God when His children do not know the things He has provided for them in Christ. We must understand that our redemption has already been obtained for us and our redemption is an eternal redemption. Our redemption is a settled fact. Satan is eternally defeated, so Satan should not be lord over us in any way.

God blesses you because His grace and love have no limit and His tender mercies are renewed every morning. We can all have God's supernatural blessing over our finances, health, emotions, and relationships because the supernatural power of God's blessing is powerful and it is God's will to bless each of us. It is God's will to bless you not because you deserve it, but because Jesus paid the price for us.

It is God's will to bless every aspect of our life, and this supernatural blessing is invoked by speaking it aloud. The blessing is the supernatural power of God in our life by the authority of Jesus' Name and the spoken Word of God. Remember, the source of any blessing is the Lord. A supernatural power is released when we bless and praise Jesus' holy name. The Bible tells us to make a joyful noise to the Lord, sing out the honor of Jesus' Name, and praise the Lord.

God's Word tells us that God places the spiritual responsibility for the family on the shoulders of the father. The role model for your children should not be your preacher, coach, teacher, or acquaintances, but the parents. Therefore, if the father does not care enough to fill the place of spiritual responsibility, then the mother and/or grandparents must fill it.

Bless your children and grandchildren, in the Name of Jesus, and release the power of God into their lives with spoken blessings. Lay your hands on them and speak healing into their spirits and minds and bodies. Speak blessings of faith, love, peace, health, wholeness, joy, laughter, happiness, confidence, and success into your children and grandchildren's lives through the power of the blessing. The parental blessing is very powerful because you have the power to speak life into the lives of your children and grandchildren. Here is an example of a blessing you can speak over your children and you can personalize it for each child:

> In the Name of Jesus, I plead the Blood of Jesus over and around _____ from the top of his/her head to the bottom of his/her feet. I claim God's blessing on _____ (name) that God will prosper him/her in everything he/she put his/her hand to. God will guard his/her heart, mind, and body and _____ will be strong in the Lord forever. I claim this in Jesus' Name. Amen

The blessing is the act of releasing the supernatural power of God into another person's life by the spoken Word of spiritual authority. As a child of God, you are entitled to His supernatural blessing. You must realize that you also have the power to hurt the lives of your children by the words that you speak to them. When you tell them that they are lazy, bums, dumb, stupid, idiots, etc., that is a curse that you are putting on your children. We can break curses on our life, but we must remember that we are to bless those that curse us, admit that others have knowingly or unknowingly spoken a curse over our lives, and identify the nature of the curses.

> I plead the Blood of Jesus over _____ and, In the name of Jesus, bind and rebuke the devil and he must flee now and take the curse with him. In Jesus Name, I claim that the curse is broken. I claim God's blessing on _____ (name) and I ask God to make him/her healthy and prosper him/her in everything he/she puts his/her hand to. God will guard his/her heart, mind, and body. I claim this in Jesus Name. Amen

Spiritually speaking, there are only two families on the earth: the family of God and the family of Satan. Every person, regardless of heritage or background, belongs to one of those two families. Which family do you belong to? The only way you can be delivered out of the family of Satan is to be born again into the family of God.

When we receive Jesus as our Savior, we have a legal right to be blessed by God. God has put all things under Jesus' feet and believers make up His body, so all principality and power has been placed under us. We have an inheritance as believers, and our redemption and authority are part of this inheritance. God has exalted Jesus far above all principality and power and might and dominion and every name that is named not only in this world but also in the world to come. The Bible tells us that the Name of the Lord is a strong tower; the righteous run to it and are safe, so Jesus' Name is a saving name.

The Rapture and Tribulation

We now live in the day of grace, and God's grace is simple. We all have a choice to believe in God, His Son and His Word or refuse to accept Jesus and stay in the darkness of the world. If we choose the world instead of God and His Son, we are turning our back on God of our own free will and we align ourselves with Satan, who is already the defeated foe of God.

If you align yourself *against* the God who created you, then you are aligning yourself on the side of Satan of your own free will. You have to be careful who or what you put as the top priority in your life. If you idolize movie stars, athletes, racing drivers, rock stars, and other celebrities, drinking, drugs, sex or put any of your personal preferences before the God of this world, you are being a friend to the world of Satan.

We all must recognize that each of us has sinned and we are disloyal to God when we do not honor and revere Him as the God of the universe. When we draw near God and humble ourselves in His presence, He will come close to us. God's love covers everybody in the world, but He will not force people to choose Him over Satan. If we think that we don't need God because we can do it on our own and we turn our back on Him, we are opening the door to the devil and his destruction.

It doesn't matter what you have done in your life. God will receive you just as you are, and He gives the restoration to favor to those who choose Him. When Christ died and was raised from the dead, He paid for every sin—past, present, and future. Nothing is required of us except believing that Jesus is the Son of God, receiving Him as our Savior, asking forgiveness for our sins, and forgiving those who have trespassed against us.

Whether you believe it or not God's Word is the law of this universe. You can deny it and you might reject it, but you cannot change the laws of the universe. You can be a nice person, but if you haven't received Jesus as your Savior and asked forgiveness for your sins, Satan has dominion over you. Without Jesus, we have no access to God and no access to heaven, so we stay in the darkness of the world under the control of Satan. Whether you believe it or not, everything in the Bible will come to pass and every one of us will have to bow down before the Lord. At that time, it will be too late to change your mind.

If you are reading this book and you have not yet received Jesus as your Savior, please do it now. God said, "My people are destroyed for lack of knowledge; because thou hast rejected knowledge, I will also reject thee. Seeing thou hast forgotten the law of thy God, I will also forget thy children" (Hosea 4:6, KJV).

We live in the day of grace where the gospel will spread throughout the world and everyone will have the opportunity to hear about Jesus. When you take Jesus as your Savior you receive: pardon, deliverance, healing, restoration, wholeness, strength, safety, and protection for every part of your life.

During the day of grace, which is the present church age, we have the opportunity to receive our salvation through the grace of God. I believe the rapture of the church is not far away, when those who believe will be taken from the world to heaven, before the tribulation on earth.

Jesus became a man so He could intercede for the human race and before Jesus left the earth He told His disciples what the signs of The End Times were. Jesus gave the church the authority and the commission to go into the world and preach the gospel to every creature, because without hearing the Word of God, a person will not believe and confess Jesus. God sent the Holy Spirit to us to help us do the job.

> We know [absolutely] that anyone born of God does not [deliberately and knowingly] practice committing sin, but the One Who was begotten of God carefully watches over and protects him [Christ's divine presence within him preserves him against the evil], and the wicked one does not lay hold (get a grip) on him or touch him. We know [positively] that we are of God, and the whole world [around us] is under the power of the

evil one. And we know [positively] that the Son of God has [actually] come to this world and has given us understanding and insight to perceive (recognize) and come to know better and more clearly Him Who is true; and we are in Him Who is true—in His Son Jesus Christ. This [Man] is the true God and Life Eternal. Little children, keep yourself from idols (false gods) [from anything and everything that would occupy the place in your heart due to God, from any sort of substitute for Him that would take first place in your life]. Amen (so let it be).

1 John 5:18–21

The Bible says that God ordained that men should be saved through the preaching of the Word of God. We need to realize what the Word of God can do through our lips, because it is our responsibility to tell people about Jesus and to do the work of God with the help of the Holy Spirit within us.

Christians are being persecuted and even killed in many countries. In the United States, the anti-Christian attitude of most news media, TV programming and talk show hosts, Hollywood movies, celebrities and directors, and even many colleges and schools are deliberately deceiving people by what they say and teach against Christians. This kind of behavior is becoming more and more prevalent in today's society because people are putting their own worldly preferences before the moral principles of the God who made them. Sign of the end-times?

When you hear of wars and insurrections (disturbances, disorder, and confusion), do not become alarmed and panic stricken and terrified; for all this must take place first, but the end will not (come) immediately. Nation will rise against nation, and kingdom against kingdom. Sign of the end-times?

When you see Jerusalem surrounded by armies, then know and understand that its desolation has come near. (Iran is trying to make bombs to use on Israel right now and most Muslim nations are against Israel. Because of satellites in space, this is the first time in history that all the prophecies in the Bible can come true, because the whole world can hear and see everything that happens in the world). Sign of the end-times?

There will be mighty and violent earthquakes, and in various places famines and pestilences, and there will be sights of terror, and great signs from heaven. (In the last few years our weather has intensified: We have had volcanoes erupting—more frequently in many different parts of the world. We have had more highly destructive earthquakes—happening more frequently than normal in many parts of the world. We have had more frequent tsunamis—that have devastated whole cities and large areas of many different countries. There are many places in the world where famine is happening, strange diseases are killing people more frequently, and pestilences and even unexplained causes have wiped out crops, flocks of birds, and large numbers of fish. Wildfires in the United States have been rapidly increasing in the last ten years and in just the first half of this year we have had more wildfires than any whole year previous.) Signs of end-times?

Luke 21:25 tells us: There will be signs in the sun, moon and stars; and upon the earth (there will be) distress (trouble and anguish) of nations in bewilderment and perplexity at the roaring and tossing of the sea.

Luke 21:31–32 tells us: When you see these things taking place, understand and know that the kingdom of God is at hand. Truly I tell you; this generation (those living at that definite period of time) will not perish and pass away until all has taken place.

Luke 21:36 tell us: Keep awake then and watch at all times (be discreet, attentive, and ready), praying that you may have the full strength and ability and be accounted worthy to escape all these things that will take place, and to stand in the presence of the Son of Man.

The Bible tells us about the Rapture of believers: For then there will be great distress, unequaled from the beginning of the world until now and never to be equaled again. If those days had not been cut short, no one would survive, but for the sake of believers those days will be shortened.

If you want to know the signs of the end times, read the Bible verses listed below: Matthew 24:3–29 below: (You can also read Luke 21:10–28, 31–36)

> While He *(Jesus)* was seated on the Mount of Olives, the disciples came to Him privately and said, Tell us, when will this take place, and what will be the sign of Your coming and of the end (the completion, the consummation) of the age?

Jesus answered them:

Be careful that no one misleads you [deceiving you and leading you into error [deception]. For many will come in (on the strength of) My name [appropriating the name which belongs to Me], saying, I am the Christ (the Messiah), and they will lead many astray. And you will hear of wars and rumors of wars; see that you are not frightened or troubled, for this must take place, but the end is not yet.

Nation will rise against nation, and kingdom against kingdom. There will be mighty and violent earthquakes, and in various places famines and pestilences and there will be sights of terror and great signs from heaven. But previous to all this, they will lay their hands on you and persecute you, turning you over to the synagogues and prisons, and you will be led away before kings and governors for My name's sake. This will be a time (an opportunity) for you to bear testimony. Resolve and settle it in your minds not to meditate and prepare beforehand how you are to make your defense and how you will answer. For I [Myself], will give you a mouth and such utterance and wisdom that all of your foes combined will be unable to stand against or refute. You will be delivered up and betrayed even by parents and brothers and relatives and friends, and [some] of you they will put to death. And you will be hated (despised) by everyone because [you bear] My name and for its sake. But not a hair of your head shall parish. By your steadfastness and patient endurance you shall win the true life of your souls. But when you see Jerusalem surrounded by armies, then know and understand that its desolation has come near. Then let those who are in Judea flee to the mountains, and let those who are inside [the city] get out of it, and let not those who are out in the country come into it; For those are days of vengeance, that all things that are written may be fulfilled. Alas for those who are pregnant and for those who have babies, which they are nursing in those days! For great misery and anguish and distress shall be upon the land and indignation and punishment and retribution upon this people. They will fall by the mouth and the edge of the sword and will be led away as captives to and among all nations; and Jerusalem will be trodden down by the Gentles until the times of the gentiles are fulfilled (completed). And there will be signs in the sun, moon and stars; and upon the earth [there will be] distress (trouble and anguish) of nations in bewilderment and perplexity [without resources, left wanting, embarrassed, in doubt, not knowing which way to turn] at the roaring (the echo) of the tossing of the sea; Men swooning away or expiring with fear and dread and apprehension and expectation of the things that are coming on the world; for the [very] powers of the heavens will be shaken and caused to totter. And then they will see the Son of Man coming in a cloud with great (transcendent and overwhelming) power and [all His kingly] glory. Now then these things begin to occur, look up and, stand up and lift up your heads, because your redemption (deliverance) is drawing near. Even so, when you see these things taking place, understand and know that the kingdom of God is at hand. Truly I tell you; this generation (those living at that definite period of time) will not perish and pass away until all has taken place. The sky and the earth (the universe, the world) will pass away, but My words will not pass away. But take heed to yourselves and be on your guard, lest your hearts be overburdened and depressed (weighed down) with the giddiness and headache and nausea of self-indulgence, drunkenness, and worldly worries and cares pertaining to [the business of] this life, and [lest] that day come upon you suddenly like a trap or a noose; for it will come upon all who live upon the face of the entire earth. Keep awake then and watch at all times [be discreet, attentive, and ready], praying that you may have the full strength and ability and be accounted worthy to escape all these things [taken together] that will take place, and to stand in the presence of the Son of Man.

After the rapture will come the seven years of tribulation on the earth, and I would not want to be left behind to go through that. We do not know how long God's grace period will last, and it is very important that we not put off asking forgiveness for our sins and receiving Jesus as our Savior because we do not want to miss God's free gift of salvation.

At that time two men will be in the field; one will be taken and one will be left. Two women will be grinding at the hand mill; one will be taken and one will be left. Watch therefore, [give strict attention, be cautious and active] for you do not know in what kind of a day [whether a near or remote one] your Lord is coming.

Matthew 24:40–42

For it is by free grace (God's unmerited favor) that you are saved (delivered from judgment and made partakers of Christ's salvation) through (your) faith. And this [salvation] is not of yourselves [of your own doing, it came not through your own striving], but it is the gift of God.

Ephesians 2:8–9

If you are reading this while it is still the day of grace, I pray that you will believe and accept God's grace for you while there is still time. God's grace is simple. Believe in the God of the Bible and His Word; receive His Son, Jesus, into your heart; ask for forgiveness for your sins; and forgive all who have trespassed against you. If you have not received Jesus as your Savior and would like to ... pray the following prayer:

Dear Heavenly Father, I believe in my heart and I confess with my mouth that God raised His Son, Jesus, from the grave for my salvation and healing, and I receive Jesus as my Lord and Savior. I ask forgiveness for my sins, and I let go of the anger and unforgiveness that I've been holding and I forgive all those who have trespassed against me. I pray in the Name of Jesus. Amen.

If you are reading this and the rapture has taken place, a new world ruler will rise to power or he might already be in power. The Bible calls him the antichrist/beast. This is my urgent testimony to you if you have missed the rapture. Pray the above prayer and resist the antichrist's system no matter what! The seven years of the tribulation will be years in which it will take some very strong conviction in order to survive. You must not follow or worship the antichrist or take his mark upon your body, and you must resist even unto death.

You must stand firm in faith, constantly believing in God and His Son, Jesus, without wavering throughout the tribulation. Jesus will return to earth at the end of the seven-year period, but you must resist the antichrist and the beast until the return of Christ at the end of the seven-year tribulation.

Conclusion

Getting acquainted with God and His Son isn't hard to do, but you have to put God first in the center of your life. You need to talk to Him, thank Him, and praise Him every day for everything good in your life: your family, a beautiful day, your good health, your home, your friends, plenty of food, your job, your finances, and for little things like helping you find you keys and so on. You will know without a doubt that He is near you when you thank Him and praise Him, because you can feel Him around you. Your faith will grow when you talk to Him and pray to Him, in Jesus Name, and study His Word.

Only then will you feel His great love and continual presence. You will see the results of you prayers and the work of His angels. You will know your Father, His Son, and His Spirit personally. You will know without a doubt that He loves you, strengthens you, warns you and guides you through your spirit, keeps His mighty angels around you, and fills you with His discernment and peace.

Please understand that the time Jesus will rapture believers from the earth is drawing near. The signs are everywhere and getting worse and more frequent every day. The days of God's Grace will be coming to an end, and if you miss the rapture, you will have to go through seven years of the terrible Tribulation, and then the end will come. If you have not drawn near to God and received His Son into your heart, I pray that you will do it now.

Eight-Week Bible Study

Week One: Getting
Acquainted with God

1. What does James 4:7–10 tell us about coming close to God?

   _____

   _____

   _____

   _____

   _____

2. What are some things you can do to help you get closer to God and His Son?

   _____

   _____

   _____

   _____

   _____

3. Read Hosea 4:6. Do you think God is telling us to come close to Him and receive what He has for us, before we are destroyed by Satan?

_____

_____

_____

_____

_____

4. What does God tell us to do in Ephesians 6:10–19?

_____

_____

_____

_____

5. What does Jesus tell us in John 10:9–11

_____

_____

_____

_____

_____

6. How does the scripture John 3:17 help us understand Jesus more?

_____

_____

_____

_____

_____

7. Read Ephesians 3:14–21 and personalize this prayer for yourself by changing the words from *you* and *your* and personalized them to *I*, *me*, and *my*. Then pray this prayer for yourself at least once a day for a week. Do you feel closer to God? Explain.

_____

_____

_____

_____

_____

8. You can also personalize Ephesians 1:17–23 if you have time.

_____

_____

_____

_____

_____

Week Two: Unwavering Faith

1. What does Hebrews 11:1, 3, 6 tell us?

    _____

    _____

    _____

    _____

    _____

2. What does 2 Corinthians 5:7 tell us, and why should we remember this?

    _____

    _____

    _____

    _____

    _____

3. What does Jesus tell us in John 10:9–11, and why is this so important?

_____

_____

_____

_____

_____

4. Read John 14:10–13. Is this telling us the Holy Spirit is working in believers as He did through Jesus when He was on earth? Why are we supposed to pray in Jesus' Name?

_____

_____

_____

_____

_____

5. How are we supposed to know what is the will of God?

_____

_____

_____

_____

_____

6. What does Mark 11:22–25 tell us about faith and why is this prayer so important?

_____

_____

_____

_____

_____

7. What are some of the things Jesus is teaching us in John 15:4–13?

_____

_____

_____

_____

_____

Week Three: Prayer and Unforgiveness

1. What does Hebrews 4:12–16 tell us to do?

   _____

   _____

   _____

   _____

   _____

2. Why is holding anger or unforgiveness harmful to us? (Mark 11:22–26)

   _____

   _____

   _____

   _____

   _____

3. What does Isaiah 53:4–5 tell us about healing?

   _____

   _____

   _____

   _____

   _____

4. Why are we supposed to pray to God in Jesus' Name? (John 16:23–28)

_____

_____

_____

_____

_____

5. Why is it helpful for more than one person to pray together? (Matthew 18:19–20)

_____

_____

_____

_____

_____

6. Why is it important for us to praise God? (Psalm 63:2–4)

_____

_____

_____

_____

_____

7. Does God always answer our prayers the way we want Him to? (Isaiah 55:8–11)

_____

_____

_____

_____

_____

Week Four: Why Healing Belongs to Us

1. What does Isaiah 53:4–5 tell us about healing?

   _____

   _____

   _____

   _____

   _____

2. What does Hebrews 4:16 tell us?

   _____

   _____

   _____

   _____

   _____

3. Why is Mark 11:22–26 so important for us to understand to get results from God?

   _____

   _____

   _____

   _____

   _____

4. Why should we never doubt that God wants us well?

_____

_____

_____

_____

_____

5. Why is holding anger or unforgiveness harmful to us?

_____

_____

_____

_____

_____

6. Tell why our praise and thanksgiving to God is so important. Psalm 105:1–8

_____

_____

_____

_____

_____

7. What does Hebrews 4:1–3 tell us?

_____

_____

_____

_____

_____

Week Five: Different Kinds of Prayers

1. How does Jesus tell us to pray in Matthew 6:5–
    15? Explain.

    _____

    _____

    _____

    _____

2. Make up your own prayer for healing of a specific
    illness.

    _____

    _____

    _____

    _____

    _____

3. Make up a prayer for a specific need.

    _____

    _____

    _____

    _____

    _____

4. Make up a prayer for your finances.

_____

_____

_____

_____

_____

5. Make up your own prayer for your family or friend.

_____

_____

_____

_____

_____

6. Make up a prayer where you plead for a person who is too young to die.

_____

_____

_____

_____

_____

7. Make up your own prayer for our nation.

_____

_____

_____

_____

_____

Week Six: Our Words are Powerful

1. What does 1 Peter 2:24 tell us? Why is this so important for you to understand?

    _____

    _____

    _____

    _____

    _____

2. What does Psalm 107:20 tell us about God's Word?

    _____

    _____

    _____

    _____

    _____

3. What do 1 John 4:4 and Revelation 12:11 tell us about the Holy Spirit?

_____

_____

_____

_____

_____

4. What does Proverbs 4:20–27 tell us about Gods Word and our walk with God?

_____

_____

_____

_____

_____

5. What does John 10:9–11 explain to us about Jesus and Satan?

_____

_____

_____

_____

_____

6. What does John 6:63 tell us about the Spirit?

_____

_____

_____

_____

_____

7. Explain what James 1:19–22 is telling us to do.

_____

_____

_____

_____

_____

Week Seven: Believers Have Authority Over Satan

1. Is there a spirit world around us? (Ephesians 6:10–12)

   _____

   _____

   _____

   _____

   _____

2. What does Ephesians 6:10–12 tell us about our enemies?

   _____

   _____

   _____

   _____

   _____

3. What does Luke 10:19–20 tell us about? How do we exercise this power?

_____

_____

_____

_____

_____

4. What weapons do we have to use against Satan? (Ephesians 6:13–18)

_____

_____

_____

_____

_____

5. What does Psalm 34:7 tell us about God's mighty angels? And Matthew 26:53?

_____

_____

_____

_____

_____

6. What does Proverbs 18:10 advise us to do for safety?

_____

_____

_____

_____

_____

7. Why is it so important that you belong to God? What in the world can harm you?

_____

_____

_____

_____

_____

Week Eight: The Rapture and Tribulation

1. What is the testimony of God regarding His Son? (1 John 5:10–11)

_____

_____

_____

_____

_____

2. What did Jesus tell His disciples in Matthew 24:3–14?

_____

_____

_____

_____

_____

3. What does Matthew 24:21–22 tell us about the rapture of believers?

_____

_____

_____

_____

_____

4. Why does Matthew 24:33–44 tell us to watch for signs?

_____

_____

_____

_____

5. What signs does Jesus tell His disciples to look for in Luke 21:7–28?

_____

_____

_____

_____

_____

6. How will we see the Son of Man coming and what will we understand? (Luke 21:31–36)

_____

_____

_____

_____

_____

7. Are you ready for the return of Jesus?

_____

_____

_____

_____

_____

e|LIVE

---

listen|imagine|view|experience

AUDIO BOOK DOWNLOAD INCLUDED WITH THIS BOOK!

In your hands you hold a complete digital entertainment package. In addition to the paper version, you receive a free download of the audio version of this book. Simply use the code listed below when visiting our website. Once downloaded to your computer, you can listen to the book through your computer's speakers, burn it to an audio CD or save the file to your portable music device (such as Apple's popular iPod) and listen on the go!

How to get your free audio book digital download:

1. Visit www.tatepublishing.com and click on the e|LIVE logo on the home page.
2. Enter the following coupon code:
   f8b6-f217-1d8a-36a0-3203-ff9c-dcd1-2d48
3. Download the audio book from your e|LIVE digital locker and begin enjoying your new digital entertainment package today!